How to Use This Book

Look for these special features in this book:

SIDEBARS, **CHARTS**, **GRAPHS**, and original **MAPS** expand your understanding of what's being discussed—and also make useful sources for classroom reports.

FAQs answer common **F**requently **A**sked **Q**uestions about people, places, and things.

WOW FACTORS offer "Who knew?" facts to keep you thinking.

TRAVEL GUIDE gives you tips on exploring the state—either in person or right from your chair!

PROJECT ROOM provides fun ideas for school assignments and incredible research projects. Plus, there's a guide to primary sources—what they are and how to cite them.

Please note: All statistics are as up-to-date as possible at the time of publication.

Consultants: Pamela Bennett, Director of the Indiana Historical Bureau; Jeremy D. Dunning, Professor of Geophysics, Indiana University; William Loren Katz

Book production by The Design Lab

Library of Congress Cataloging-in-Publication Data
Stille, Darlene R.
 Indiana / by Darlene R. Stille.
    p. cm.—(America the beautiful. Third series)
 Includes bibliographical references and index.
 ISBN-13: 978-0-531-18582-7
 ISBN-10: 0-531-18582-6
 1. Indiana—Juvenile literature. I. Title. II. Series.
 F526.3.S75 2008
 977.2—dc22   2007043670

©2009 Scholastic Inc.
All rights reserved. Published in 2009 by Children's Press, an imprint of Scholastic Inc.
Published simultaneously in Canada. Printed in the United States of America.
SCHOLASTIC, CHILDREN'S PRESS, and associated logos are trademarks and/or registered trademarks of Scholastic Inc.

1 2 3 4 5 6 7 8 9 10 R 18 17 16 15 14 13 12 11 10 09

Indiana

BY DARLENE R. STILLE

Third Series

Children's Press®
An Imprint of Scholastic Inc.
New York ★ Toronto ★ London ★ Auckland ★ Sydney
Mexico City ★ New Delhi ★ Hong Kong
Danbury, Connecticut

CONTENTS

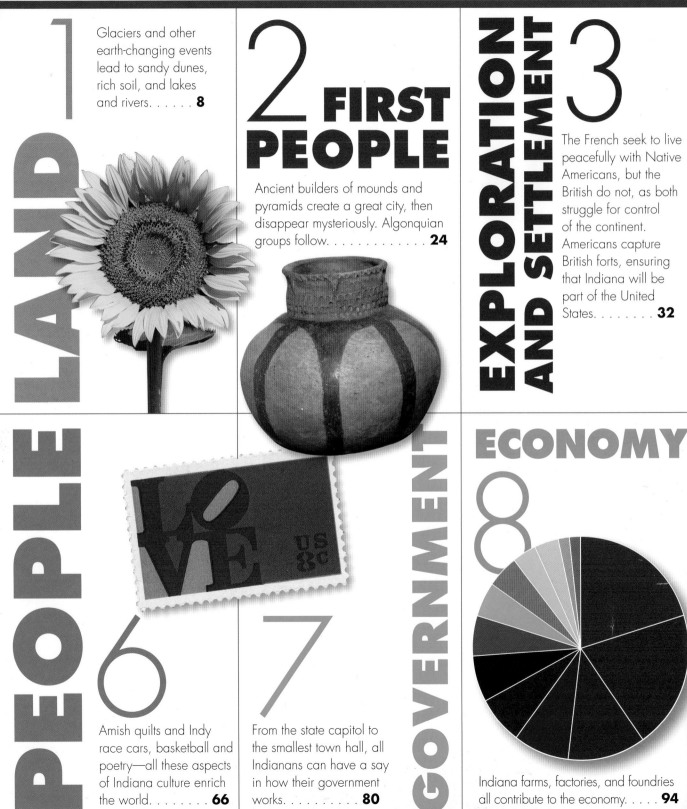

GROWTH AND CHANGE

4

Automobiles and railroads combine to make Indiana a giant of industry and "the Crossroads of America." **42**

MORE MODERN TIMES

5

With the tremendous output of Indiana industries, the United States contributes to the Allied victory in World War II. In the second part of the century, Indiana learns to meet the challenges of changing times. **56**

9 TRAVEL GUIDE

Climb a sand dune, explore a cave, watch a car race, or step back in time at a living history museum—you can do it all in Indiana. **102**

PROJECT ROOM

★

LAKE MICHIGAN

MICHIGAN

National New York Central Railroad Museum

SOUTH BEND

GARY

Indiana Dunes National Lakeshore

National College Football Hall of Fame

Hoosier Buggy Shop

Kankakee

Maumee

FORT WAYNE

Foellinger-Freimann Botanical Conservatory

Jasper-Pulaski State Fish and Wildlife Area

Quilters Hall of Fame

Wabash

LAFAYETTE

MUNCIE

OHIO

ILLINOIS

INDIANA

Ernie Pyle State Historic Site

INDIANAPOLIS

Indiana State Capitol

TERRE HAUTE

Indiana University

Eiteljorg Museum of American Indians and Western Art

BLOOMINGTON

West Fork White

East Fork White

Ohio

George Rogers Clark National Historical Park

Marengo Cave National Landmark

KENTUCKY

Wabash

NEW ALBANY

Lincoln Boyhood National Memorial

EVANSVILLE

Ohio

Wyandotte Caves State Recreation Area

0 — 30
Miles

QUICK FACTS

State capital: Indianapolis
Largest city: Indianapolis
Total area: 36,418 square miles (94,322 sq km)
Highest point: Hoosier Hill, 1,257 feet (383 m), in Wayne County
Lowest point: Along the Ohio River, 320 feet (98 m)

LAKE
ERIE

PENNSYLVANIA

Welcome to Indiana!

HOW DID INDIANA GET ITS NAME?

Indiana means "land of the Indians," but the name was originally applied to a place different from the state of Indiana. British traders in the 1760s gave this name to some land farther east that they had received from Native Americans. Virginia, however, claimed to own the land and added the first "Indiana" to its territory. After the Revolutionary War, the new United States named the land west of the Ohio River the Indiana Territory. When new states were carved from this territory, one of them was named Indiana.

INDIANA

WEST VIRGINIA

VIRGINIA

KENTUCKY

READ ABOUT

A meadow at West
Beach, Indiana
Dunes National
Lakeshore

CHAPTER ONE

LAND

★

I N INDIANA, SAND DUNES LINE THE LAKE
MICHIGAN SHORE, AND IN THE CENTER
OF THE STATE, FIELDS OF CORN AND
SOYBEANS STRETCH TO THE HORIZON. The
southern end of the state boasts steep hills and
limestone caves. Overall, the 36,418 square
miles (94,322 square kilometers) that make up
Indiana are pretty level. The highest point, in
Wayne County along the Ohio border, is Hoosier Hill at 1,257 feet (383 meters) above sea
level. The lowest point, in the southwest where
the Wabash River flows into the Ohio River, is
320 feet (98 m) above sea level.

Indiana Topography

Use the color-coded elevation chart to see on the map Indiana's high points (orange) and low points (green to dark green). Elevation is measured as the distance above or below sea level.

Elevation	
Feet	Meters
1,100	335
900	274
700	213
500	152

0   30 Miles
0   30 Kilometers

PREHISTORIC ICE

Indianans can thank prehistoric ice sheets called glaciers for making much of their state look the way it does today. Ice covered Indiana as far south as Martinsville several times in the distant past. The last ice age in Indiana began about 700,000 years ago. As the climate became colder, ice crept slowly south from what is now Michigan to where Indianapolis is today. When the climate warmed, the glaciers **receded**. The last ice age ended in Indiana 10,000 to 12,000 years ago.

The glaciers made drastic changes to the land. The ice mowed down forests and rocky hills. It pushed dirt and gravel into river gorges and valleys. It ground up rocks that would become rich soil. The glaciers and melting ice created Lake Michigan, one of the five Great Lakes, and smaller lakes and rivers in Indiana. The largest of these smaller lakes is Lake Wawasee between South Bend and Fort Wayne.

Earthquakes in Indiana? They happen once in a while. A 1909 quake between Terre Haute and Vincennes knocked down chimneys and shook pictures from walls.

WORD TO KNOW

receded *pulled or moved back over time*

Indiana Geo-Facts

Along with the state's geographical highlights, this chart ranks Indiana's land, water, and total area compared to all other states.

Total area; rank . . . . 36,418 square miles (94,322 sq km); 38th
   Land; rank . . . . 35,867 square miles (92,895 sq km); 38th
   Water; rank . . . . 551 square miles (1,427 sq km); 39th
   Inland water; rank . . . . .316 square miles (818 sq km); 43rd
   Great Lakes; rank . . . . 235 square miles (609 sq km); 8th
Geographic center . . . . Boone County, 14 miles (23 km)
                                         north-northwest of Indianapolis
Latitude . . . . 37° 47' N to 41° 46' N
Longitude . . . . 84° 49' W to 88° 4' W
Highest point . . . . Hoosier Hill, 1,257 feet (383 m), in Wayne County
Lowest point . . . . .Along the Ohio River, 320 feet (98 m)
Largest city . . . . Indianapolis
Longest river .Wabash, 475 miles (764 km)

Rhode Island, the nation's smallest state, would fit inside Indiana 23 times!

Corn is harvested on an Indiana farm.

LAND REGIONS

Four states and Lake Michigan border Indiana. Michigan and Lake Michigan are to the north. Ohio is to the east. The Ohio River separates Indiana from Kentucky, the state to its south. The Wabash River separates Indiana from Illinois, the state to its west. Within Indiana lie three main land regions: The Great Lakes Plains, the Till Plains, and the Southern Hills and Lowlands.

The Great Lakes Plains

The Great Lakes Plains form a strip of fertile lowland across northern Indiana that also stretches across southern Michigan, northern Illinois, southern Wisconsin, and into northwest Ohio. In the central Great Lakes

Plains, glaciers left behind many small lakes, ridges, and small hills called drumlins. The rich soil in the southern part of Indiana's Great Lakes Plains makes good farmland.

The Till Plains

The Till Plains are a band of deep, rich soil across the center of Indiana, beginning in Kansas and Nebraska and stretching to western Ohio. Indiana's Till Plains seem almost flat.

The Southern Hills and Lowlands

The Southern Hills and Lowlands are in south-central Indiana. Glaciers never arrived to grind down this part of the state, which has more hills and valleys than any other part of Indiana. Underground streams have carved out several caves. The soil in the Southern Hills and Lowlands is not as rich as in other parts of Indiana. But the area does have deposits of coal and oil.

FAQ

Q: CAN THE SAND DUNES ALONG LAKE MICHIGAN MOVE?

A: "Live" dunes can move several feet a year. Wind blows a few sand grains that bump other sand grains and make them fly up into the air. The wind then blows these sand grains into other sand grains. The leapfrogging sand grains make a dune slowly move.

A waterfall at McCormick's Creek State Park

Hoosiers shovel out after a snowstorm in Carmel.

CLIMATE

All of Indiana has a moderate climate, but the weather can be very different in the northern and southern parts of the state. Warm, moist air blows up from the Gulf of Mexico to help make the southern parts of Indiana warmer than the northern parts. Summer days in Evansville in the south are hot and humid. Evansville's average daily high temperature in July is 89 degrees Fahrenheit (32 degrees Celsius). South Bend in the north has a lower average daily high in July of 83°F (28°C).

Winters tend to be more severe in the north. Evansville, in the south, might get 13 inches (33 centimeters) of snow in a year, while Michigan City on Lake Michigan can get more than 20 inches (51 cm) in just a day or two. As cold air passes over the warmer waters of the big lake, it makes the water evaporate, forming clouds that drop snow along the shore. Strong winds can blow these "lake effect" snow clouds from Gary to South Bend and even to Elkhart. In the plains area of Indiana, powerful thunderstorms can flare up in the spring and summer.

TRAGIC TORNADOES

Indiana is on the edge of what is called "tornado alley," a region that is mainly in the Great Plains states. Warm, moist air blowing over the flat plains from the Gulf of Mexico sometimes collides with cold dry air coming down from the Arctic. Thunderstorms fire up where the two air masses meet. In the most powerful thunderstorms, winds start to swirl and form a funnel—a tornado. Sometimes the tornado touches down on the ground and, like a giant vacuum cleaner, it can suck up cars, tear off roofs, and flatten houses.

FLOODS

Heavy rains sometimes cause Indiana rivers to flood. Indiana's worst flooding occurred in 1913 along the Whitewater River, a **tributary** of the Miami River in Ohio. Between 5 and 9 inches (13 and 23 cm) of rain and sleet fell during two days in March. Some 90 people died as a result of the flood. Flooding along the Ohio River in 1937 also caused great damage to Indiana towns along the river from the Ohio border to Illinois.

WORD TO KNOW

tributary *a smaller river that flows into a larger river*

Residents sort through the wreckage after a tornado in Newburgh.

Weather Report

TEMPERATURE 116°F

TEMPERATURE -36°F

This chart shows record temperatures (high and low) for the state, as well as average temperatures (July and January) and average annual precipitation for Indiana.

Record high temperature . . . . .116°F (47°C) at Collegeville on July 14, 1936
Record low temperature . . . .–36°F (–38°C) at New Whiteland on January 19, 1994
Average July temperature . . . . 75°F (24°C)
Average January temperature . . . . 27°F (–3°C)
Average yearly precipitation . . . . 40 inches (102 cm)

Source: National Climatic Data Center, NESDIS, NOAA, U.S. Dept. of Commerce

Indiana's most destructive tornadoes to date struck the northern and central parts of the state in April 1965. Eleven tornadoes touched down in 20 counties. Swirling winds and flying debris killed 137 people and injured more than 1,700 others.

PLANT LIFE

Many of the plants found in Indiana are the kinds seen in most midwestern fields, forests, and backyards. Oak, maple, black walnut, hickory, ash, beech, elm, and sycamore trees grow in the forests that cover about one-fifth of the state. Prairie wildflowers of central Indiana include milkweed, aster, sunflowers, and black-eyed Susans. Plants more typical of a warm, wet climate grow in extreme southern Indiana, where bald cypresses tower more than 100 feet (30 m) above the water of Goose Pond and Twin Swamps Nature

Sunflower

Grasses grow along a pond at Hoosier National Forest.

Preserve in Posey County. Insect-eating plants, such as the pitcher plant, grow in bogs and other wetlands all over the state.

ANIMAL LIFE

From swampy lands near the Ohio River to windblown beaches along Lake Michigan, Indiana is home to all kinds of wildlife. Rainbow trout flash through inland streams. Perch, bass, catfish, and sunfish fill Indiana's

More than 1,100 native plants live among the sand dunes of Indiana's Lake Michigan shore.

Many river otters make their home in Indiana's wooded areas.

ENDANGERED ANIMALS

Indiana wildlife specialists are working hard to save the state's endangered animals. Among the animals in danger are the Karner blue butterfly, the Indiana bat, the eastern puma, and the piping plover. Bald eagles, peregrine falcons, and river otters once faced extinction. Indiana biologists have had success breeding these animals in captivity and then releasing them back to their natural habitats in Indiana.

Karner blue butterfly

many lakes. Squirrels, raccoons, otters, mink, and badgers share the wooded areas with deer. Birds such as cardinals, sparrows, finches, and woodpeckers perch on trees and soar through the skies. In harvested fields, wild turkeys, pheasants, and grouse peck at leftover grain in the fall.

HUMANS AND THE ENVIRONMENT

The growth of industry that brought jobs to Indiana in the late 19th century also caused lasting problems. To this day, coal-burning factories and power plants around Indianapolis and other cities continue to cause air pollution. Steel mills, oil refineries, and factories along

Lake Michigan and rivers leading to the lake produce large amounts of mercury and other dangerous chemicals. Some of these chemicals are dumped into the lake. Since about 1990, the state has done a lot to clean up the steel mill areas. But Indianans continue to struggle with balancing the need to protect the environment against the need of industry to produce profits and create jobs.

THINK ABOUT IT!

Pollution

Some Indianans say that tough environmental rules will drive up prices and make it harder for Indiana companies to compete. In October 2007, the Indiana Air Pollution Control Board voted 11–1 to adopt minimum federal mercury limits, or caps. The board also voted to allow coal-burning power plants that give off large amounts of mercury to buy pollution credits from plants that stay below the mercury cap. Thus, the polluting plants can buy the right to pollute from plants that produce less pollution. Many people who work in the energy industry argue that allowing some pollution is necessary to keep energy prices down.

But one member of the Indiana Air Pollution Control Board, Philip S. Stevens, voted against the new rules. "Given the known **toxicity** of mercury and the known health effects—especially on children and pregnant women—and increasing scientific evidence that mercury gets into the environment and spreads in ecosystems quickly, I felt [a] stronger rule was appropriate," he said. And Zoe Lipman of the National Wildlife Federation points out, "Even in Indiana, which relies heavily on coal for electricity, . . . we can significantly reduce mercury emissions for about the cost of a cup of coffee [per Indiana household] a month."

WORD TO KNOW

toxicity *the degree to which something is poisonous*

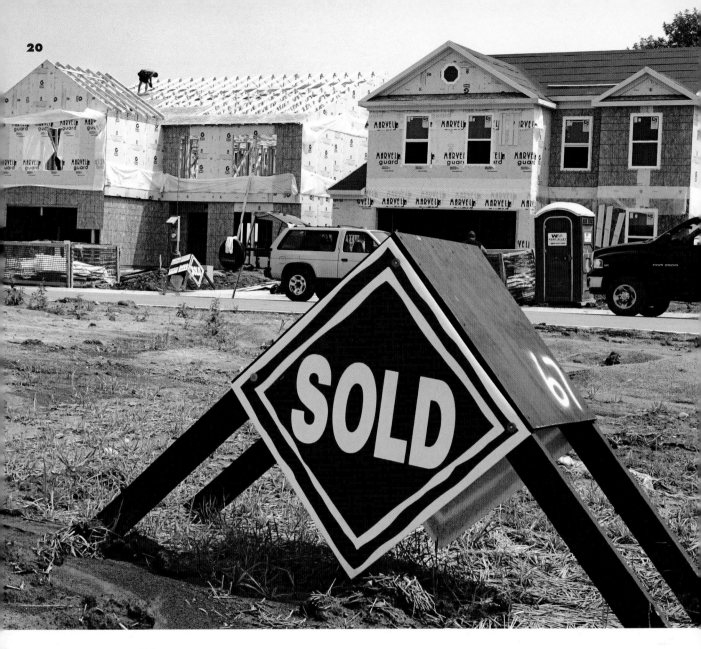

Land is cleared to build housing developments such as this one in Noblesville.

WORD TO KNOW

urban sprawl *the spread of a city and its suburbs into rural areas*

Another environmental challenge that Hoosiers must deal with is **urban sprawl**. This spread of housing developments, industry, and shopping centers into rural areas chops up large areas of land into smaller areas. Plants and wildlife need a certain amount of space in order to live, but sprawl has broken up the land into areas that may be too small for wild plants and animals to survive.

SAVING THE DUNES

Sprawl and pollution have long threatened the dunes along Lake Michigan. The struggle to save the dunes began in the late 1800s, when steel mills and factories first brought wealth and jobs to the area. As a result of the development, however, many dunes were destroyed.

Indiana made a small part of the dunes a state park in 1926, but soon companies wanted to build more steel mills around the park. Many people worked to stop them, including schoolteacher Dorothy Richard Buell, who organized people to buy

A view of a factory from the beach at the Indiana Dunes National Lakeshore

MINI-BIO

DOROTHY RICHARD BUELL: HERO OF INDIANA'S DUNES

Dorothy Buell (1886–1977) was born in Wisconsin but enjoyed summers at her family cottage in Ogden Dunes, Indiana. Later, she and her husband moved to Ogden Dunes. She became president of the Save the Dunes Council and worked tirelessly to round up volunteers, raise funds, and get national leaders to help. Without her, there might never have been an Indiana Dunes National Lakeshore.

? **Want to know more?** See www.savedunes. org/history/earliest_efforts/dorothy_buell/

Indiana National Park Areas

This map shows some of Indiana's national parks, monuments, preserves, and other areas protected by the National Park Service.

LAKE MICHIGAN

MICHIGAN

Michigan City

Gary

South Bend

Indiana Dunes NL

Kankakee

St. Joseph

Maumee

Tippecanoe

Fort Wayne

St. Marys

ILLINOIS

Wabash

Mississinewa

Lafayette

Muncie

OHIO

National Park area

NHP — National Historical Park
NL — National Lakeshore
NMEM — National Memorial

Indianapolis

Terre Haute

Eel

Whitewater

Bloomington

0 — 30 Miles
0 — 30 Kilometers

Lake Monroe

W. Fk. White

E. Fk. White

Vincennes
George Rogers Clark NHP

Jasper

Ohio

Wabash

Patoka

Lincoln Boyhood NMEM

N
W E
S

Evansville

KENTUCKY

Ohio

land around the park. She also convinced national leaders, such as U.S. senator Paul H. Douglas, that the dunes should be saved.

In a 1959 speech, Douglas said, "I can only emphasize that if these mills are built here, with the industrial city that will grow up around them, not only will the Dunes be destroyed, but the little state park will itself be made virtually unusable because of the pollution of air and water." Douglas helped get Congress to establish the Indiana Dunes National Lakeshore between Gary and Michigan City, even though he was a senator from Illinois, not Indiana. He saw the dunes as both a regional and national treasure. The national park that Buell, Douglas, and others helped establish preserves 15,000 acres (6,700 hectares) of dune land along 15 miles (24 km) of lakeshore.

SEE IT HERE!

THE SMOKIN' DUNE

From far away, it looks as if smoke is blowing off the top of Mount Baldy, a sand dune in the Indiana Dunes National Lakeshore that is 123 feet (37 m) tall. In fact, the "smoke" is sand that the wind has picked up from the top of the dune. Mount Baldy is a "live" dune that moves away from Lake Michigan at the rate of 4 to 5 feet (1.2 to 1.5 m) each year.

A backpacker sets out for a hike at Indiana Dunes National Lakeshore.

c. 10,000 BCE

The first people arrive in Indiana

▲ **c. 1000 BCE**

People in Indiana begin to make pottery

800 BCE

The Adena culture develops in the Ohio River valley

CHAPTER TWO

FIRST PEOPLE

★

ABOUT 12,000 YEARS AGO, THE FIRST PEOPLE ENTERED THE LAND THAT IS NOW INDIANA. Where did they come from? Their ancestors may have crossed a land bridge between Asia and today's Alaska. Later, the waters of the Bering Sea covered the land bridge. These ancient people kept moving south, and some came to what is now the midwestern United States. Scientists call these ice age people Paleo-Indians.

200 CE ▲
People in Indiana begin to hunt with bows and arrows

c. 1000
Mississippians arrive in Indiana

1450
Angel Mounds is abandoned

These archaeologists investigate the discovery of mastodon remains near Hebron.

WORD TO KNOW

archaeologists *people who study the remains of past human societies*

ICE AGE HUNTERS

Not many Paleo-Indians lived in ancient Indiana, and they left few clues behind. **Archaeologists** have found only some spear points, knives, scrapers, and other stone tools along riverbanks.

The Paleo-Indians moved around as they hunted large mammals, such as mammoths, mastodons, and giant sloths. Over thousands of years, the climate grew warmer, and big forests of oak, hickory, and other hardwood trees began to grow. The large mammals disappeared, forcing the Paleo-Indians to hunt smaller game, such as deer.

FIRE MAKERS

About 6,000 years ago, the culture of Indiana's people began to change. A time that scientists call the Archaic period began. Archaic people may have come up to Indiana from farther south. Like the Paleo-Indians, they probably lived in small groups and moved from place to place. But the Archaic people discovered ways to make life better. They found that mussels in the Wabash and Ohio rivers were easy to get and good to eat. Archaeologists have found piles of mussel shells they left behind.

But the real revolution was that the Archaic people learned how to cook food. They roasted meat over a fire and boiled food in pots made of animal skins by heating rocks in a fire and putting the hot rocks into water-filled pots. They also learned to prepare certain foods for winter.

Archaeologists in 2006 found one of their prehistoric "kitchens" at Charlestown State Park in Clark County. In this 4,000-year-old kitchen, the Native Americans made oil from hickory nuts. They crushed and ground up the nuts between big slabs of rock, and then boiled the nuts to get the oil, which they could store for later use.

THE FIRST MOUND BUILDERS

Another time of great progress began about 3,000 years ago, when ancient people learned to make pottery. Beginning about 100 BCE, they lived in villages of 100 to 1,000 people and traded with other Native Americans far away. Archaeologists have discovered 45 sites of ancient villages in what are now Martin, Lawrence, and Jackson counties alone. In these villages, oval-shaped houses made of wooden poles covered with bark and hides were grouped in a circle around a central plaza.

FAQ

Q8 HOW DID ICE AGE PEOPLE MAKE TOOLS OUT OF STONE?

A8 They hit a rock called chert with a harder rock to chip off pieces, forming spear points, knives, and other tools.

Native arrowheads

This painting depicts a harvest ceremony at a Hopewell mound.

Archaeologists have found the remains of dogs in burial grounds, indicating that the Mound Builders kept dogs, perhaps to help with hunting or as pets.

The people also built huge mounds of dirt and rocks. The largest one in Indiana is a circular mound that is 6 feet (2 m) high and 360 feet (110 m) in diameter. Most mounds were for burials, but some may have been places to hold ceremonies. Among the first Mound Builders were the people of the Adena culture, which arose in the Ohio River valley in about 800 BCE. The Adena people built thousands of mounds in Indiana and Ohio. They were mainly hunter-gatherers, but they also grew squash, gourds, and pumpkins.

Meanwhile, another group of Mound Builders came to Indiana from the Ohio Valley around 100 BCE. Archaeologists call them the Hopewell. The Hopewell may have grown out of the Adena culture. The Hopewell people traded with other people far away. They had copper from Lake Superior and seashells from the Gulf of Mexico. They made jewelry and decorated pottery with these materials. The Hopewell people began to disappear from Indiana around 500 CE. What happened to them is a mystery.

Between 200 and 800 CE, people in Indiana began to grow fields of corn and squash. They also learned to hunt with bows and arrows.

PYRAMID BUILDERS

A new group of people began arriving in Indiana around 1000 CE. Archaeologists call them Mississippians. Each Mississippian group had a chief. The chief and other leaders lived in large towns surrounded by fields of corn, beans, and squash. The largest Mississippian settlement in Indiana was at what is now Angel Mounds State Historic Site in Evansville. Several thousand people lived there in houses with walls made of earth and covered with tall, thatched roofs. People of the Mississippian culture also built a number of smaller towns along the Ohio and Wabash rivers.

SEE IT HERE!

ANGEL MOUNDS STATE HISTORIC SITE

What was life like in Indiana's biggest town 800 or 900 years ago? See for yourself at Angel Mounds State Historic Site in Evansville. Archaeologists have been digging up and studying the 500-acre (200 ha) site for about 60 years. Indoor exhibits show how the Mississippian people lived. You can also take a guided hike around the grounds to see models of their earth homes with thatched roofs (below).

Picture Yourself . . .

Living in a Mississippian Town

You live with your parents, brothers, and sisters in a one-room home. All the houses in your village are built around an open area. If you are a girl, you help plant corn, beans, squash, and other crops in the spring. Your mother teaches you how to grind corn in a big wooden pot with a big wooden stick so the grain can be stored in underground pits. She also teaches you how to cook by roasting food over a fire or baking it in underground ovens. If you are a boy, you learn how to fish with nets and hunt with a bow and arrows. Sometimes your family gathers with the other village families in the center square to watch games or see the chief lead a ceremony to mark the change of seasons.

DIGGING UP THE PAST

Glenn A. Black (1900–1964), who was born in Indianapolis, was the first archaeologist to study the mounds in Indiana left by prehistoric people. In the early 1930s, he went to work for the Indiana Historical Society, and he was Indiana's only archaeologist until 1960. He identified or **excavated** about 5,000 sites, including Angel Mounds. When Indiana University established an archaeological laboratory in 1971, it was named in his honor.

WORD TO KNOW

excavated *removed soil and rock from an area to dig up buried items*

An Algonquian birch-bark canoe

Indiana's Mississippian towns were part of a great civilization that began in what is now Mississippi and Alabama and spread north to Wisconsin and Minnesota. In each Mississippian town was a plaza where people gathered for ceremonies. Each town also had at least one earth mound or a pyramid with a flat top. A temple or the chief's house sat on top of the pyramid. By 1450, Mississippians had abandoned Angel Mounds and other sites. Archaeologists are still trying to figure out why the Mississippian culture disappeared.

ALGONQUIANS

Some Mound Builders stayed in Indiana, but they did not plant crops or live in towns. They became hunter-gatherers again.

Soon a few people from the Algonquian group of Native Americans began moving in from the east. The Algonquians were a group of nations including Miamis, Delawares, Kickapoos, Potawatomies, and Shawnees, who all spoke a similar language. They lived in villages, planting crops in spring and summer and hunting animals in winter. Miamis had moved into Indiana to get away from the Iroquois, who attacked them. Miamis were also the first Native Americans in Indiana to meet European explorers, who reached the area in 1679.

Native American Peoples

(Before European Contact)

This map shows the general area of Native American peoples before European settlers arrived.

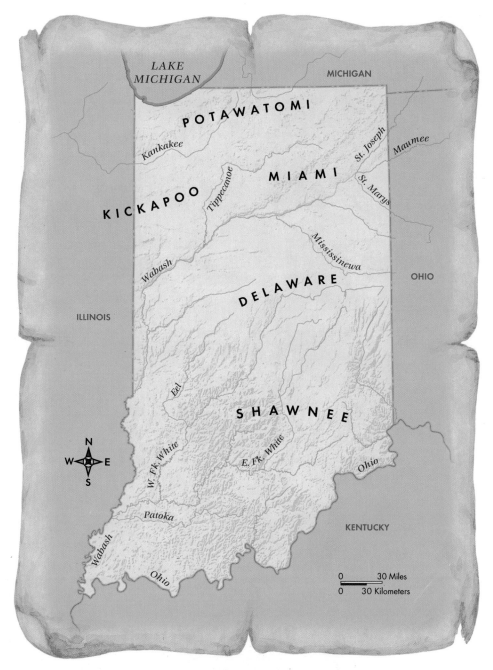

LAKE MICHIGAN

MICHIGAN

POTAWATOMI

Kankakee

St. Joseph

Maumee

MIAMI

St. Marys

KICKAPOO

Tippecanoe

Mississinewa

Wabash

OHIO

DELAWARE

ILLINOIS

Eel

SHAWNEE

N W E S

W. Fk. White

E. Fk. White

Ohio

Patoka

KENTUCKY

Wabash

Ohio

0   30 Miles

0   30 Kilometers

1679 ►

René-Robert Cavelier,
Sieur de La Salle, explores
northern Indiana

1732

The French found
Vincennes, Indiana's
first permanent
European settlement

1763

The British take
over New France

EXPLORATION AND SETTLEMENT

★

IN THE 1500s, THE FRENCH BEGAN TO SETTLE IN WHAT IS NOW CANADA. They claimed all the land around the Great Lakes for the French king. French explorers crossed Lake Michigan into what would become Illinois, Michigan, and Indiana. Fur traders and priests followed them. French traders offered Native Americans beads, metal pots, guns, and other goods in exchange for the valuable furs. The priests tried to convert the Native Americans to Christianity.

1779 ▶

George Rogers
Clark recaptures
Fort Sackville

1783

Indiana becomes
part of the
Northwest Territory

1787

Congress passes the
Northwest Ordinance

European Exploration of Indiana

The colored arrows on this map show the routes taken by explorers between 1670 and 1680.

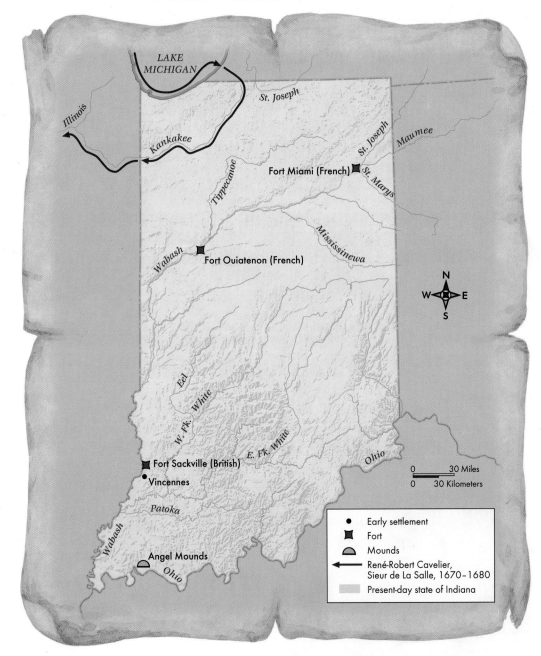

LAKE MICHIGAN

Illinois

Kankakee

St. Joseph

St. Joseph

Maumee

St. Marys

Tippecanoe

Fort Miami (French)

Fort Ouiatenon (French)

Wabash

Mississinewa

Eel

W. Fk. White

E. Fk. White

Ohio

Fort Sackville (British)

Vincennes

Patoka

Wabash

Angel Mounds

Ohio

N
W E
S

0	30 Miles
0	30 Kilometers

● Early settlement

⚑ Fort

⌓ Mounds

← René-Robert Cavelier, Sieur de La Salle, 1670–1680

 Present-day state of Indiana

RENÉ-ROBERT CAVELIER, SIEUR DE LA SALLE: DARING EXPLORER

René-Robert Cavelier, Sieur de La Salle (1643–1687), was a Frenchman who sought fame and fortune in Canada. Native Americans told him of great rivers to the south. La Salle thought they might lead to the Pacific Ocean. From there, he could travel to Asia, where he could earn a fortune by trading in silks and spices. He explored what became Ohio, Indiana, and Illinois and traveled the Mississippi River to the Gulf of Mexico. The following year, he tried to reach the mouth of the Mississippi by sea, but his ships landed on the coast of what is now Texas. His crew members were angry because they ran out of food and water, and many died or deserted. Those who remained killed him because they believed him to be incompetent and arrogant.

? Want to know more? See www.civilization. ca/vmnf/explor/lasal_e2.html

Ships used in the expedition of René-Robert Cavelier, Sieur de La Salle

THE FIRST EUROPEAN EXPLORERS

The first Europeans to see Indiana were French explorers René-Robert Cavelier, Sieur de La Salle, and his expedition of 12 men. He explored northern Indiana in 1679 and 1680. One of La Salle's men described the weather as they traveled along the shore of Lake Michigan: "As we were approaching land our boat was at one time full of water; afterwards it was overset and we lost our entire equipment. . . . For three days we lived only upon acorns which we found under the snow." La Salle and his group paddled their canoes down the St. Joseph River to the south bend in the river. Today, the place where they landed is the city of South Bend.

La Salle claimed Indiana for France, and it became part of a territory that the French called Louisiana. Louisiana also included land from the Great Lakes region to the Gulf of Mexico.

Q8 HOW COULD SOMEONE CROSS LAKE MICHIGAN IN A CANOE?

A8 French fur traders built giant canoes up to 40 feet (12 m) long. Native Americans showed them how to stretch the bark of a birch tree over a cedar frame. The giant canoes were strong and light. They could hold 3 tons of furs or goods for trading and could carry 12 people.

INDIANA'S FUR TRADE

The French began to set up trading posts in Indiana in the early 1700s. The first post was called Fort Ouiatenon (we-ah-tay-NO), on the Wabash River near Lafayette. In 1732, they founded a post farther south at Vincennes, which became Indiana's first city.

Although these settlements were French, people from a variety of races lived and worked in them. The first people of African heritage in Indiana may have been enslaved persons brought in by French fur traders. Slavery was illegal in France, but it was not outlawed in New France. Fur traders owned both Africans and Native Americans. At least one trader was a free, or not enslaved,

Inside a trading post

African. He was Jean Baptiste Point du Sable. In the 1770s, du Sable operated a trading post at the mouth of Trail Creek, in what is now Michigan City, before moving on to what became Chicago.

The French traders and the Native American trappers usually enjoyed a mutually beneficial relationship. French traders often married Native American women and made gestures, such as giving gifts, to show friendship. The traders sold the furs to merchants who made coats and hats for people in Europe, where beaver fur was fashionable. The French became wealthy on the fur trade.

Picture Yourself . . .

at Fort Ouiatenon

Your father is a French fur trader. Your mother belongs to the Miami Nation. You live in a log cabin outside a fort at this busy trading post. You play with Indian children in their village nearby. You speak French with your father and Algonquian with your mother. If you are a girl, you do chores around the family's log cabin, helping your mother cook, making clothing from cloth or animal skins, and planting corn and squash in the fields around the fort. Your mother has also taught you to sew pieces of birch bark together to make the outer covering of canoes. If you are a boy, you help your father build the cedar frames for canoes. Later, you will travel with your father to Native American villages to trade for furs.

Replica of Fort Ouiatenon

THE BRITISH TAKE OVER

Meanwhile, trouble was brewing between France and Britain, which had established colonies in the East. The British wanted to get in on the fur trade. They were also rivals with France for control of North America. War broke out between the British and the French in 1754. Americans call the conflict the French and Indian War, because many Native Americans were **allies** of the French. The Native peoples who traded with the French allied themselves with the French. In 1763, the war ended in defeat for the French. They gave the British all their lands in Canada and along the Ohio River, including the land that would become Indiana.

The British approach to colonization of land created conflicts with the Native Americans. The British, unlike

New France, the part of North America claimed by France before 1673, extended from eastern Canada to the Rocky Mountains and south to the Gulf of Mexico.

WORD TO KNOW

allies *people who are on the same side in a conflict*

MINI-BIO

PONTIAC: BRAVE WARRIOR

A leader of the Ottawa nation, Pontiac (1720?–1769) united the Native American groups of the Great Lakes and the Ohio Valley. He led a rebellion in 1763 to get rid of the British, and his Native American forces captured many British forts. He had hoped that France would become an ally and help him fight its old enemy, the British, but the French did not. Pontiac realized that he could not win his war alone, so he made peace with the British. A Native American killed Pontiac at a religious center in Cahokia, in what is now southern Illinois, but no one knows why.

Want to know more? See www.ohiohistorycentral.org/entry.php?rec=306

the French, wanted to take Indian lands, settle them, and displace the Indians from them. Native Americans rose up against the British in 1763.

After suffering many defeats by Native Americans, the British government made peace and ordered their colonists not to move west of the Appalachian Mountains. The colonists, however, ignored this order and kept moving westward. To punish the colonists, the British paid Native Americans to raid colonial settlements. The British did not keep control for long, however.

INDIANA AND THE REVOLUTIONARY WAR

In 1776, the American colonies declared independence from Great Britain. In the Revolutionary War that followed, Native Americans in Indiana supported the British.

Virginian George Rogers Clark went on a secret mission to capture British forts in Illinois and Indiana. With only about 200 men, mostly pioneer farmers, he captured forts at Kaskaskia and Cahokia on the Mississippi River in southern Illinois. Most people living at the forts were French and did not like the British, so they did not put up much of a fight. Some went with Clark to capture Fort Sackville at Vincennes. The French at Vincennes also gave up the fort without a fight. Clark left a small number of soldiers at Fort Sackville and returned to Kaskaskia.

George Rogers Clark's troops had to wade through high waters to reach Vincennes.

The British were furious. They marched from Fort Detroit, which today is the city of Detroit, Michigan, and easily recaptured Fort Sackville. It was December 1778, and the British commander let the troops go home for the winter. In the spring, they planned to come back and attack Kaskaskia.

When Clark learned that the British had recaptured Fort Sackville, he did not wait for good weather to return. He and his soldiers set off right away. At some points, the men had to wade through flooded rivers in freezing water that was up to their chests, holding their long rifles over their heads to keep them dry. They ran out of food. After 18 days, they reached Vincennes. They built fires, dried out their clothes, and had something to eat. Now they were ready to take back Fort Sackville.

The surrender of Fort Sackville in 1779

FAQ

Q8 WHAT STATES WERE CREATED OUT OF THE NORTHWEST TERRITORY?

A8 The territory was eventually carved into the states of Ohio, Indiana, Illinois, Michigan, and Wisconsin.

Clark tricked the British into thinking that he had a large army by digging trenches around the fort and by ordering his soldiers to march waving flags and making enough noise for at least 600 troops. The Americans, who were deadly marksmen, shot at the British. Clark also began to dig tunnels into the fort. All of this activity frightened the British into surrendering.

The Americans held the forts in Indiana during the Revolutionary War. Clark's military victories were important contributions toward the Americans winning all the British lands between the Appalachian Mountains and the Mississippi River when the war ended in 1783. The new nation named these lands the Northwest Territory.

The U.S. government rewarded Clark and his soldiers with land in what would become the state of Indiana. The soldiers founded the first American settlement in Indiana, a town called Clarksville. In 1787, Congress passed the Northwest Ordinance, a document that divided the rest of the Northwest Territory into townships and sections. The ordinance stated that as many as five states would be created from the Northwest Territory and that an area could become a state once it had 60,000 settlers.

Arthur St. Clair became the Northwest Territory's first governor, and Marietta, in what is now Ohio, became the capital. When St. Clair arrived in Marietta in 1788, the town faced constant attacks by Native Americans, who had never surrendered the land. St. Clair demanded that the Native Americans give up the entire Ohio Valley. When he tried to bribe Native American leaders, they became enraged. They began to prepare for war.

SEE IT HERE!

GEORGE ROGERS CLARK NATIONAL HISTORICAL PARK

A park and memorial in Vincennes honor the feat of George Rogers Clark in driving the British from Fort Sackville. The memorial is a large, round building. Inside it are seven murals that tell the story of how Clark captured the fort. Every summer, the National Park Service offers rides on the Wabash River in a big canoe, from which visitors can see the fort as French fur trappers did.

The Ohio River near Marietta

1795

The Treaty of Greenville gives lands in Indiana to the United States

1800

Indiana Territory is created

1816 ▶

Indiana becomes the 19th state

CHAPTER FOUR

GROWTH AND CHANGE

★

WITH ALL THEIR BELONGINGS PILED ON RAFTS, COLONISTS POLED AND FLOATED ALONG THE OHIO AND WABASH RIVERS. They came to settle the land of Indiana. Native Americans watched the settlers arrive, fearing that the settlers would take even more land.

1847

Indiana's first railroad is built

1889

Standard Oil decides to build a refinery in Whiting

1911 ▲

First Indianapolis 500 race is held

A scene from the Battle of Tippecanoe in 1811

WORD TO KNOW

confederation *an association of groups that comes together with common goals*

THE FINAL BATTLES

The trouble began in Ohio. A **confederation** of Algonquian groups, led by the great Miami leader Little Turtle, began attacking the settlers. President George Washington sent 1,400 soldiers in 1790 to destroy Indian villages in Indiana and western Ohio. Little Turtle lured the soldiers into a trap near Fort Wayne and defeated them. The next year, Washington sent in 2,000 poorly trained troops, and the Native Americans defeated this force, too.

Finally, in 1794, Washington had General Anthony Wayne assemble an army of 3,000 seasoned fighters. Wayne—who had earned the nickname "Mad Anthony" for his reckless bravery during the Revolutionary War— was ordered to destroy the Algonquian confederation and their way of life.

After being driven back by Wayne's forces when he attacked a fort near the Indiana border, Little Turtle realized the Native Americans could not defeat Wayne, so he urged peace talks. The confederation, however, replaced him with another leader, Turkey Foot, who was willing to fight on. The two sides fought a great battle at a place called Fallen Timbers near Toledo, Ohio, and the U.S. troops overwhelmed the Native Americans. Admitting defeat, 1,100 Indian leaders, including Little Turtle, signed the Treaty of Greenville in 1795, handing most of Ohio to the United States in exchange for other land in the Northwest Territory.

In 1800, Congress divided the Northwest Territory into the Indiana Territory and the Ohio Territory. Vincennes was made the capital of Indiana Territory, and William Henry Harrison became its governor. Following the land acquisition policy of the federal government, Harrison had soon persuaded and pressured Native Americans to sell land in Indiana. He helped make it possible for settlers to buy the land on credit.

Tecumseh

A great Shawnee leader named Tecumseh did not believe that anyone could buy or sell land. "Sell a country!" he wrote in a letter to Harrison. "Why not sell the air, the clouds and the great sea, as well as the earth? Did not the Great Spirit make them all for the use of his children?" Tecumseh and his brother, called the Prophet, tried to form another confederation to fight the settlers. Harrison attacked and destroyed their meeting place, a settlement called Prophetstown (near present-day Lafayette), at the Battle of Tippecanoe in 1811.

Tecumseh joined with the British against the Americans when another war broke out, called the War of 1812. Harrison finally defeated Tecumseh's warriors in the Battle of the Thames in Canada. Tecumseh was killed. Almost all the Native Americans then left Indiana. The Potawatomies remained. In the 1830s, they, too, were forced to leave the state.

SETTLEMENT AND STATEHOOD

New settlers in Indiana Territory came mostly from southern states and Ohio. Rufus Easton, an early settler, encouraged people to come to the new territory, saying "there neither is, nor in the nature of things can there ever be, anything like poverty there. . . . Every person, however poor, may with moderate industry become in a very short time a land holder."

Such descriptions must have sounded especially tempting to African Americans wanting to escape from enslavement in the southern states. The Northwest Ordinance prohibited slavery in the territory. But land speculators and slaveholders asked Congress to change this law and permit slavery as a way of attracting more white settlers. They also flooded the territorial legislature with **petitions** asking that slavery be made legal. Congress and the territorial lawmakers refused these demands.

WORD TO KNOW

petitions *written calls for action, usually with signatures of people who support the action*

A family of settlers in the late 1800s

Indiana: From Territory to Statehood

(1800–1816)

This map shows the original Indiana territory and the area (in yellow) that became the state of Indiana in 1816.

1818 Treaty Line

Lake of the Woods

Lake Superior

British Possessions

Illinois Territory, 1809

Mississippi

Missouri Territory, 1812

Lake Michigan

Lake Huron

Michigan Territory, 1805

Lake Erie

0   100 Miles

0   100 Kilometers

Illinois

INDIANA 1816

OHIO 1803

Mississippi

Wabash

Vincennes

Ohio

Corydon

VIRGINIA 1788

KENTUCKY 1792

Legend:
- Northwest Territory
- Indiana Territory, 1800
- Indiana Territory, 1809
- States
- Other territories
- State of Indiana, 1816
- ★ Territorial capitals

SEE IT HERE!

NEW HARMONY

This village on the Wabash River near Evansville was founded in the early 1800s by a group of deeply religious German Americans called Harmonists, who wanted to create a perfect society through hard work, **frugal** living, and prayer. In 1825, they sold their successful town to a group led by social reformer Robert Owen that believed in social equality for everyone. The second group soon quarreled among themselves, and the community broke up. In the 1930s, the state of Indiana bought the town and turned it into a living history museum. Today, you can see what life was like in the 1800s as a tour guide tells about New Harmony's history.

WORD TO KNOW

frugal *careful with money*

The steam locomotives on Indiana's first trains burned wood and pulled cars that looked like stagecoaches.

Although it remained illegal, slavery did not die in Indiana—it just changed its name. When Governor Harrison arrived in the territory with slaves, he called them indentured servants. These were people who willingly signed on to work for a master without wages, in exchange for food and shelter. Many slaveholders who moved to Indiana followed his example.

In 1803, Indiana became the first territory to pass a law restricting the rights of African Americans. The "Black Law" prohibited testimony by people of color against whites in court. The territory passed additional laws that prevented black men from voting, being elected to office, or serving in the militia.

In 1816, Indiana became the 19th state. Slavery was illegal according to the 1816 state constitution. This document also made the state largely responsible for providing a public education system.

Indiana's first state capital was Corydon, which in 1813 had replaced Vincennes as the territory's capital. But lawmakers had set aside land for a new capital in the center of the state. It would be called Indianapolis, meaning "city of the Indians."

ROADS AND RAILROADS

Indianapolis grew slowly because it was hard to get there. Rivers at that time were the best transportation routes, but the White River flowing past Indianapolis was too shallow for boats. The few roads in Indiana were awful. In some areas, people on foot had to slog through bogs and marshes. Horses and riders could fall into the sticky mud. Wagons and stagecoaches sometimes got stuck in deep ruts or overturned when they hit a big rock or a tree stump.

Things got a little better when the National Road reached Indianapolis in 1831. This gravel road, which

The arrival of a train at the depot in Michigan City

led from Maryland to Missouri, was the first road built with federal funds. Pioneers in covered wagons rumbled westward over the National Road. Some settled on the rich farmlands of central Indiana. In the 1830s, Indiana built the north-south Michigan Road connecting the Ohio River with Lake Michigan, so that these farmers could transport their crops to market.

These early roads still made for slow going. A lawyer who often traveled the Michigan Road on horseback wrote in 1833, "I had many a hard ride with the mud so deep that 15 or 20 miles [24 or 32 km] were a good day's journey." Over time, more and better roads were built.

It was the coming of the railroads, however, that helped Indiana become "the Crossroads of America." In 1847, a railroad with a steam-powered locomotive began operating between Madison and Indianapolis. Soon, seven other major railroads were running through Indianapolis. By 1880, railroad tracks zigzagged everywhere throughout the state.

FAQ

Q8 WHAT HAPPENED TO THE NATIONAL ROAD?

A8 The National Road through Indiana eventually became U.S. Route 40, which went from Atlantic City, New Jersey, to San Francisco, California. The interstate highway system replaced much of Route 40, especially in the West.

LEVI COFFIN: ANTISLAVERY ACTIVIST

Born in North Carolina, Quaker Levi Coffin (1798–1877) strongly believed that slavery was immoral and should be ended. Indiana's Underground Railroad received an enormous boost in 1826 when Levi and his wife, Catharine, settled in Newport. They hid African Americans in secret rooms for weeks at a time so that they could rest and regain strength for the journey. During 20 years in Indiana, the Coffins helped some 2,000 enslaved persons escape. The Coffins moved to Cincinnati, Ohio, in 1847 and helped another 1,300 African Americans. Levi's work earned him the nickname President of the Underground Railroad.

? Want to know more? See www.nps.gov/history/nr/travel/underground/in2.htm

WORDS TO KNOW

abolitionists *people who work to end slavery*

secede *to withdraw from a group or an organization*

THE UNDERGROUND RAILROAD AND THE CIVIL WAR

In the 19th century, Indiana's free black settlers faced hostility from many of their white neighbors. In fact, in 1851, the second state constitution barred people of color from entering or settling in Indiana. Other whites, such as a religious group known as the Quakers, were friendly toward African Americans. Some white Indianans were **abolitionists**, people who believed that slavery was wrong and should be abolished.

Thousands of enslaved African Americans bravely escaped from their owners in the South and headed for freedom in Northern states or Canada. It was a dangerous journey. In 1850, the U.S. Congress passed the Fugitive Slave Law, which stated that escaped slaves captured in Northern states would be returned to their Southern owners. Abolitionists developed the Underground Railroad, a system for helping and hiding the runaways. A number of free black and white Hoosiers helped the runaways by giving them food, clothing, and places to hide. "Conductors" guided the escaped slaves from one "station," or hiding place, to another on the Underground Railroad.

By 1860, Southern slave states, afraid the U.S. government would abolish slavery, began to **secede** from the

Union. They formed a new nation that they called the Confederate States of America.

When the Civil War broke out in 1861, Indiana sided with the Union, because Hoosiers wanted to keep the United States together. Indiana sent more than 200,000 soldiers of both races to fight. One Civil War battle was fought in Corydon, when Confederate troops crossed the Ohio River from Kentucky. In 1863, these 2,500 Confederate soldiers led by General John Hunt Morgan entered Indiana. Some 450 members of the Harrison County Home Guard failed to stop them. Morgan's Raiders spent six days plundering Corydon and other places in seven Indiana counties. The Raiders finally crossed into Ohio, where Union soldiers defeated them. Over the course of the war, nearly 25,000 soldiers from Indiana gave their lives to preserve the Union.

The Third Indiana Cavalry in 1864

AUTOS AND OIL

When the Civil War ended in 1865, most Indianans, also known as Hoosiers, still made their living by farming. Two developments soon led Indiana to change from a rural state to an industrial powerhouse: the discovery of oil and the invention of automobiles.

The Standard Oil Company discovered oil and natural gas deposits in central Indiana and neighboring Ohio in the late 1880s. The company needed to build a refinery to process the gas and oil into kerosene for lamps and, later, gasoline for automobiles. The refinery had to be close to rail and water transportation. Standard

FAQ

Q8 WHERE DID THE TERM "HOOSIER" COME FROM?

A8 No one is really sure. Folktales give a wide range of origins, from "who's here?" to "whose ear?" to "husher" and more. Some historians suspect it comes from an ancient Anglo-Saxon word meaning "hill dweller."

MINI-BIO

EUGENE V. DEBS: UNION ORGANIZER

Eugene V. Debs (1855–1926) was a union organizer and founder of the Socialist Party in America. As president of the American Railway Union, he led a strike against the company that made Pullman passenger cars. For his role in the strike, he was sent to prison. He ran as the Socialist Party candidate for U.S. president five times between 1900 and 1920. His home in Terre Haute is a National Historic Landmark and a museum.

? Want to know more? See www.ohiohistorycentral.org/entry.php?rec=117

WORDS TO KNOW

union *an organization formed by workers to try to improve working conditions and wages*

strike *an organized refusal to work, usually as a sign of protest about working conditions*

interurbans *small trains or trolley cars connecting two or more cities*

Oil executives in 1889 chose Whiting, on the shore of Lake Michigan. The lake and three railroads provided easy transportation to the area.

In addition, the location was close to Chicago, the biggest city in the Midwest. Thousands of people moved into Whiting to build and operate the huge refinery.

Nearby, in 1908, the United States Steel Corporation built the world's largest steel mill. The company built housing for its workers and founded the city of Gary. It was named after U.S. Steel's chairman, Elbert Gary. The state made a good gathering place for the key ingredients used in making steel. Boats carried iron ore from Minnesota. Trains brought coal from Illinois and Pennsylvania. Other steel mills and foundries opened in neighboring East Chicago.

Electric train lines were also set up in the early 1900s to carry passengers between cities in Indiana. The trains were called **interurbans**, and they connected Muncie, Terre Haute, Indianapolis, and other Indiana cities and towns. With the coming of the automobile, all the interurbans, except the South Shore Line connecting South Bend to Chicago, disappeared.

Indiana's automobile industry began in South Bend at the Studebaker Manufacturing Company. Studebaker was the world's largest maker of horse-drawn wagons

The first Memorial Day race at the Indianapolis Motor Speedway, May 30, 1911

before it began making electric automobiles in 1902 and gasoline-powered vehicles in 1904. Other automakers set up shop in Indiana. Indiana craftspeople built fine-quality luxury autos and by 1909 produced more cars than any other state except Michigan. Businessman Carl Fisher built the Indianapolis Motor Speedway in 1906, to give pioneering automakers a track to test out new models. It soon became a popular place to hold auto races. The first Indianapolis 500 race was held at the speedway in 1911.

A group of schoolchildren in Gary, early 1900s

High wages paid to maintain the railroads lured many German immigrants to Michigan City in northwestern Indiana in the late 1800s. They earned $1.00 per day.

IMMIGRATION

Between 1880 and 1920, millions of immigrants poured into the United States, looking for jobs and political and religious freedom. They came from Ireland, Germany, Italy, and Mexico, as well as eastern Europe and Asia. They braved long, hard journeys by ship over the Atlantic and Pacific oceans. They flocked to the steel mills, foundries, and factories that were opening up in Gary and other new cities in northwestern Indiana. Most newcomers did not speak English. They were willing to take even the most dangerous jobs.

The population of Indianapolis exploded, from fewer than 19,000 residents in 1860 to almost 234,000 by 1910. Adding to the growth was the migration of African Americans from southern states. African Americans, like members of other ethnic groups, lived together in their own neighborhoods. They formed their own social clubs and published their own newspapers. In 1884, George Knox began to publish the *Indianapolis Freeman* to spread his views on **civil rights** and the duties of citizenship.

The first African American woman millionaire was Madam C. J. Walker, who in 1910 chose Indianapolis as the place to build a factory for making her hair care products. She was impressed with the city's many railroad lines that went all over the country. She was also impressed with the size of its black community.

MINI-BIO

MADAM C. J. WALKER: MILLIONAIRE

Madam C. J. Walker (1867–1919) was born Sarah Breedlove on a plantation in Louisiana. This daughter of former enslaved parents won fame and success by making and selling a line of hair products for African American women. In 1910, she moved to Indianapolis and built her factory there. She was a major contributor to a YMCA for the city's African American youth and to other African American causes. The Madame Walker Theatre Center in Indianapolis is dedicated to African American arts and culture.

? Want to know more? See www.greatwomen.org/women.php?action=viewone&id=163

WORLD WAR I

Hoosiers again answered the call of their country when the United States entered World War I in 1917. The smoke-belching furnaces and factories in East Chicago, Gary, and Whiting began turning out weapons and vehicles for war. The United States sent more than 4.3 million men and women to fight the war. Almost 117,000 were killed, including about 1,400 from Indiana.

By the time the war ended in 1918, Hoosiers, like other Americans, were tired of the fighting. They were glad to go back to making steel and automobiles and farming the land. They hoped for many years of peace and prosperity.

WORD TO KNOW

civil rights *basic human rights that all citizens in a society are entitled to, such as the right to vote*

1929

The stock market crashes

1933

One-quarter of Hoosier workers are unemployed

1920s ▲

The Ku Klux Klan is prominent in Indiana

MORE MODERN TIMES

★

AFTER WORLD WAR I, HOOSIERS LEFT FARMS TO WORK IN THE GROWING CITIES. For the first time, more Hoosiers lived in the cities than in the countryside. In homes, schools, and businesses, electricity replaced kerosene lamps. With the arrival of electricity came new electric appliances. Soon Indiana became a leading maker of electric stoves, refrigerators, and radios.

1959

Steel workers go on strike

1967 ▶

Richard G. Hatcher is elected the first black mayor of Gary

2003

The Indiana Commission on Hispanic/Latino Affairs is created

58

Members of the Ku Klux Klan wore white robes and hoods and terrorized African Americans and other citizens.

WORD TO KNOW

Prohibition *a legal ban on the making or sale of liquor*

THE KLAN IN INDIANA

An increasing number of African Americans came to Indiana seeking jobs during World War I. The Ku Klux Klan soon followed. The Klan was a violent group formed originally in the South to drive former slaves back to white control after the Civil War. In the 1920s, it expanded its hate list to include immigrants, Catholics, Jewish people, union members, political radicals, and those who opposed **Prohibition**.

In Indiana, the Klan claimed to be the voice of American patriotism, and the Indiana chapter became one of the most powerful Klan groups in the country. An estimated 40 percent of white males in Indiana in the 1920s were Klan members. The Klan leader, a wealthy man named David Curtis Stephenson, supported political candidates who helped the Klan take over Indiana politics. In 1925, however, Stephenson was convicted of murdering a woman. After he was sent to prison, the Klan began to lose power in Indiana.

THE ROARING TWENTIES

The 1920s was a time of prosperity for many people in Indiana and all over the United States. The economy was strong. The value of **stocks** was soaring, and some people became rich in a short time. People later called it the Roaring Twenties.

Americans fell in love with the automobile. Wealthy people especially loved the fine cars made in Indianapolis, Auburn, and other towns in Indiana. They rode to picnics at the Indiana Dunes in stately Cole Touring Cars. They drove to Indianapolis offices in Studebakers. They dashed off to football games in South Bend in the sporty Cord or Stutz Bearcat.

Hoosiers listened to jazz, the new rage in music, at clubs like the Black Orchid in Indianapolis. Phonographs and radios brought great jazz musicians such as Louis Armstrong and Fats Waller right into Indiana homes. Hoosiers also loved to see films showing in the big, new movie palaces. They cheered for the Notre Dame football team, coached by the legendary Knute Rockne.

KNUTE ROCKNE: LEGENDARY FOOTBALL COACH

Knute Rockne (1888–1931) brought fame to the University of Notre Dame fighting Irish football team by winning 105 games between 1918 and 1930. He was born in Norway and attended Notre Dame, where he became a star football player. The school asked him to stay on as football coach. He urged his team to victory by asking them to "win one for the Gipper." That referred to George Gipp, a star player on Rockne's team who had died of pneumonia in 1920 during his senior year and became a legend and folk hero.

? **Want to know more?** See www.collegefootball.org/famersearch.php?id=20038

WORD TO KNOW

stocks *monetary investments in a company*

A top-of-the-line Duesenberg auto could cost as much as $25,000 in the 1920s, compared with a Model T Ford, which cost about $300. In those days, a doctor earned only about $3,000 a year.

1913 Stutz Bearcat

A team of horses is auctioned off by a farmer, near Montmorenci, during the Great Depression.

THE GREAT DEPRESSION

In 1929, stock prices fell rapidly, and many banks went out of business. Much of the world entered a time called the Great Depression. This era brought hard times for the 3.2 million people living in Indiana. Farmers were especially hard-hit. Prices for farm products had been low during the 1920s, and many Indiana farmers had borrowed money. As prices fell even lower during the Depression, farmers could not pay back the money.

Some lost their farms. Steel mills and factories laid off workers or shut down. Few people could afford expensive cars, so most Indiana companies that made them went out of business. By 1933, about one-quarter of all Indiana workers were unemployed, and many families became homeless.

In 1933, the U.S. government began programs created to help people. One, the Works Progress Administration (WPA), aimed to put Hoosiers back to work. Many Hoosiers worked on WPA projects that improved the state's bridges, roads, and highways. Under other programs, artists painted murals on the walls of more than 40 post offices in Indiana.

HOOSIERS AND WORLD WAR II

The Great Depression started to lift when World War II began in 1939 and the United States began producing war equipment for its allies. The United States entered the war in 1941, after Japanese warplanes bombed the U.S. naval fleet at Pearl Harbor in the Hawaiian Islands. The nation needed soldiers and sailors. It also needed tanks, guns, ammunition, ships, and airplanes. Almost 400,000 Indiana men and women joined the armed forces. Black Hoosiers such as Charles "Buster" Hall joined the Tuskegee Airmen, the first African Americans trained as warplane pilots. Factories and foundries in northwestern Indiana worked around the clock turning out war supplies. Women workers took the jobs of men who went overseas. "I was paid an unbelievable thirty-five dollars a week!" said Virginia Mayberry of Middlebury.

By the time the war ended in 1945, about 400,000 members of the U.S. armed forces had died in the fighting. Almost 12,000 of them were from Indiana.

POSTWAR INDIANA

Hoosiers went back to their daily lives after the war ended. The world was changing, however. Better roads, along with more and better cars, allowed people to live farther from their jobs. Suburbs with new homes and big yards grew up around Indianapolis and other cities. Most people who moved from the cities to the suburbs were white. Meanwhile, African Americans continued moving to Indianapolis, Gary, and other northern cities for jobs. They made up a growing percentage of the urban population. Many African Americans had nowhere to live but run-down neighborhoods. Sometimes, the discrimination they faced led to outbreaks of violence.

Towns such as Elwood, shown here, grew larger after World War II.

A street fair in Gary

During the World War II years, more jobs had opened to people of color, and the number of African Americans in Indiana had doubled. With the increased population came more political power. In 1941, Robert Lee Brokenburr became the first African American to serve in the Indiana Senate. But the big change came in 1967, when Richard G. Hatcher was elected mayor of Gary. Hatcher gained national prominence as a spokesman for urban African Americans.

MINI-BIO

RICHARD G. HATCHER: PIONEERING BLACK MAYOR

Richard G. Hatcher (1933–), born in Michigan City, graduated from Indiana University and Valparaiso University School of Law. In 1967, he became the first African American mayor of Gary and one of the first black mayors of a major U.S. city. He won reelection five times and served as mayor for 20 years. After stepping down as mayor, he became an author and college professor.

? Want to know more? See www.iun.edu/~cra/newsletter/fall1997.shtml

THIS PLANT ON STRIKE USA - CIO

INDIANA TODAY

Beginning in the 1960s and 1970s, some factories moved out of the state. Many, including the Studebaker Corporation, closed down. Many steel mills in northwestern Indiana closed or laid off workers. The number of steelworkers in Gary dropped from about 30,000 in the late 1960s to fewer than 6,000 by 1987. Some people thought labor unrest was partly to blame for the closing of steel mills. Workers belonged to the United Steelworkers Union, which fought for better wages and working conditions. When the steel companies refused to meet workers' demands, the workers often went on strike. After a long strike in 1959, when steel mills cut production by 90 percent, their customers began buying steel made in other countries.

Thousands of unemployed whites moved out of Gary, Hammond, and other northwestern Indiana cities. At the same time, the percentage of African Americans in the cities increased. More than 85 percent of Gary's residents were African American by the 2000s, the highest percentage of black residents of any U.S. city. Many of them were poor and unemployed.

By 2000, some 25 percent of the almost 800,000 residents of Indianapolis were black. Indiana's suburban areas continued to gain population, mainly as a result of white people leaving the city centers.

Newcomers were still arriving in Indiana during the early 2000s. Between 2000 and 2006, Indiana added almost 39,000 new residents a year. Many of them came from Mexico, Puerto Rico, and other Spanish-speaking

FAQ ★ ★ ★

Q8 WHAT IS THE TALLEST BUILDING IN INDIANA?

A8 The 48-floor Chase Tower in Indianapolis, built in 1990 and rising to almost 830 feet (253 m), is the tallest building in the Midwest outside of Chicago.

Inside the Indianapolis City Market

regions. Between 1990 and 2000, Indiana's Hispanic population grew by more than 117 percent. In 2003, the governor's office created the Indiana Commission on Hispanic/Latino Affairs (ICHLA) to ensure economic, educational, and social equality for the newest wave of Hoosier immigrants.

Hoosiers are working to meet the challenges of today and tomorrow. Many communities have plans to attract new residents and new businesses, especially high-tech companies. Hoosiers take great pride in their state and are determined to keep Indiana the "Crossroads of America."

READ ABOUT

A day at the
Porter County
Fair in Valparaiso

PEOLE

PEOPLE

★

HOOSIERS COME FROM A WIDE RANGE OF BACKGROUNDS AND CULTURES. Germans are the largest ethnic group, accounting for almost 23 percent of Indiana's population. The next-largest groups are Irish and English. Indiana is also home to people of African and Hispanic heritage, as well as people from France, Russia, Poland, and other parts of eastern Europe.

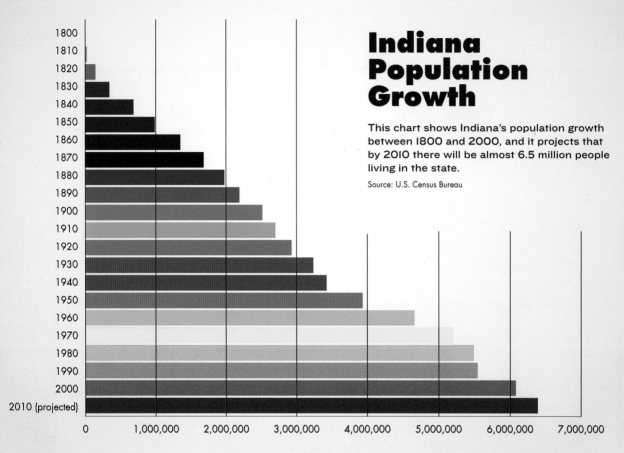

Indiana Population Growth

This chart shows Indiana's population growth between 1800 and 2000, and it projects that by 2010 there will be almost 6.5 million people living in the state.

Source: U.S. Census Bureau

People QuickFacts

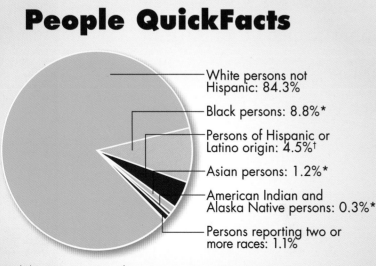

- White persons not Hispanic: 84.3%
- Black persons: 8.8%*
- Persons of Hispanic or Latino origin: 4.5%†
- Asian persons: 1.2%*
- American Indian and Alaska Native persons: 0.3%*
- Persons reporting two or more races: 1.1%

*Includes persons reporting only one race
†Hispanics may be of any race, so they are also included in applicable race categories
Source: U.S. Census Bureau, 2005 estimate

HOOSIER ROOTS

People are still immigrating to Indiana. The 2000 census showed that about 187,000 Indiana residents came from other countries. Of these, 23 percent came from Europe, 27 percent from Asia, and 41 percent from Latin America, mainly Mexico. But despite a mix of ethnic groups, Indiana has a smaller percentage of minorities than many other

Where Hoosiers Live

The colors on this map indicate population density throughout the state. The darker the color, the more people live there.

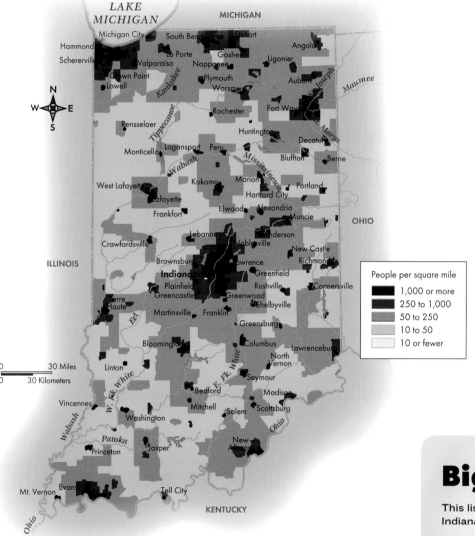

People per square mile

- 1,000 or more
- 250 to 1,000
- 50 to 250
- 10 to 50
- 10 or fewer

states. About 89 percent of all Hoosiers are white, compared with about 75 percent for the United States as a whole. Fewer than 9 percent of Hoosiers are black, and 4.5 percent are Latinos.

Big City Life

This list shows the population of Indiana's biggest cities.

Indianapolis	785,597
Fort Wayne	248,637
Evansville	115,738
South Bend	104,905
Gary	97,715

Source: U.S. Census Bureau, 2006 estimates

MINI-BIO

JAMES WHITCOMB RILEY: DOWN-HOME POET

Born in Greenfield, James Whitcomb Riley (1849–1916) captured the language of Indiana's country folk, the people he grew up with. He based beloved characters such as "The Raggedy Man" and "Little Orphant [sic] Annie" on a hired hand and an orphan girl who helped out on the family farm. When he was young, Riley traveled around, painting signs and helping a medicine salesman. He sent his first poems to newspapers under the name Benjamin F. Johnson of Boone. His poems developed a worldwide following. He moved to Indianapolis and earned his living by traveling around giving poetry readings.

? **Want to know more?** See www.indianahistory.org/pop_hist/people/riley.html

HOW TO TALK LIKE A HOOSIER

Hoosier is just another word for *Indianan*. Residents call Indiana the "Hoosier State," and they proudly call themselves Hoosiers, a term that has meant someone or something from Indiana since at least 1826. If you run into trouble on the Indiana Toll Road, a Hoosier Helper tow truck is likely to stop and give you a hand.

Some Hoosiers speak in a distinct way. Indiana poet James Whitcomb Riley tried to capture that sound in his poem "The Old Swimmin'-Hole," which was published in 1883:

*"Oh! the old swimmin'-hole! whare the crick so still and deep
Looked like a baby-river that was laying half asleep,
And the gurgle of the worter round the drift jest below
Sounded like the laugh of something we onc't ust to know."*

HOW TO EAT LIKE A HOOSIER

Hoosiers enjoy corn on the cob, melons, and other fresh fruits and vegetables sold at Indiana farm stands. Pork from Indiana hogs—in the form of sausages or the pork chops sold at the state fair—is very popular. In southern Indiana, Hoosiers love pies made from locally grown persimmons or sweet potatoes. In central and northern Indiana, they savor meat-and-potato dinners as their European ancestors once did.

Watermelon

Corn on the cob

20 astronauts or space flight trainees have attended the College of Engineering at Purdue University in West Lafayette. Hoosiers don't have to live in Bloomington or West Lafayette to attend these state-run schools, because there are branches in Richmond, Kokomo, Gary, Mishawaka, Hammond, and many other communities.

Students from all over the world come to South Bend to study at the University of Notre Dame. This Roman Catholic school is ranked among the top 20 U.S. schools in areas such as architecture, business, chemistry, and philosophy.

MINI-BIO

PERCY JULIAN: CHEMICAL GENIUS

Percy Julian (1899–1975), who was born in Montgomery, Alabama, did not take his opportunity to study science at DePauw University in Greencastle lightly. He was the grandson of a slave whose right hand was mutilated as punishment for learning to read. Julian went on to earn a doctorate in chemistry from the University of Vienna in Austria. He invented an artificial version of the hormone cortisone—which greatly reduced the price of this drug for people suffering from arthritis—and a drug to treat glaucoma, an eye condition. As a pioneering African American scientist, he served as a mentor and inspiration to the next generation of black students wanting a career in science.

? **Want to know more?** See www.pbs.org/wgbh/nova/julian

TALENTED HOOSIERS

Hoosier writers of note include Gene Stratton-Porter, who set her novel *Freckles* in central Indiana, and Meredith Nicholson, who wrote both poetry and prose. *A Hoosier Chronicle* is one of his best-selling works.

Hoosiers have created some of the best-loved characters in children's books. Hoosier author and illustrator Norman Bridwell created Clifford the Big Red Dog. Raggedy Ann and Andy came from the imagination of cartoonist Johnny Gruelle. Annie Fellows Johnston created the Little Colonel. *Garfield*, one of the most popular cartoon strips of all time, sprang from the drawing board of Jim Davis, who was born in Marion.

W★W

Many U.S. astronauts were born or grew up in Indiana, including Joseph P. Allen, Frank Borman, Ken Bowersox, Anthony W. England, Kevin A. Ford, Virgil "Gus" Grissom, Jerry Ross, Janice E. Voss, Charles D. Walker, Donald Williams, and David Wolf.

Television host David Letterman is joined by his mother, Dorothy Mengering, at the ribbon cutting for the David Letterman Communication and Media Building at Ball State University in Muncie.

MINI-BIO

COLE PORTER: MASTER OF THE MUSICAL

One of America's greatest songwriters, Cole Porter (1891–1964), born in Peru, wrote popular songs with witty lyrics and beautiful melodies. He composed the music and wrote the words to songs for musicals such as Paris and Kiss Me, Kate. His list of hit songs includes "I've Got You Under My Skin," "Just One of Those Things," and "I Love Paris."

❓ **Want to know more?** See www.pbs.org/wnet/americanmasters/database/porter_c.html

Many actors came from Indiana. James Dean, who played restless youths in the 1950s, was born in Marion. Carole Lombard, an early motion-picture star, was born in Fort Wayne. Steve McQueen, a star of the 1960s and 1970s, was born in Beech Grove. TV personality David Letterman and broadcaster Jane Pauley were both born in Indianapolis.

PERFORMING ARTS

Gary gave the music world some of its biggest pop stars in the talented Jackson family. First came the 1970s phenomenon, the group of brothers known as the Jackson 5. Later, several Jacksons became stars on their own, including Michael, and sisters Janet and La Toya. Other Hoosier music stars include John Mellencamp and Crystal Gayle.

Indiana has outstanding fine arts performers as well. Violinist Joshua Bell was born in Bloomington and has won the Avery Fisher Prize for outstanding achievement. Classical musicians have come from all over the United States and the world to perform with the Indianapolis Symphony Orchestra. Local musicians bring their violins, cellos, and oboes to try out for spots with one of Indiana's several community orchestras, such as the Northwest Indiana Symphony Orchestra or the Richmond Symphony Orchestra. Many communities have youth orchestras and competitions to encourage up-and-coming young musicians. Twyla Tharp, one of the world's most accomplished modern dance **choreographers**, was born in Portland.

FOLK ART AND FINE ART

A Hoosier named Marie D. Webster wrote books in the first half of the 20th century that helped make the craft of quilting popular, with patterns that feature poppies, daisies, tulips, and sunflowers. Her home in Marion became the headquarters of the Quilters Hall of Fame.

Amish women also make exquisite hand-stitched quilts by piecing together fabrics of different colors into geometric patterns with names such as log cabin and wedding ring. A religious group that originally came from Switzerland, the Amish believe in hard work and in living a simple life, shunning such modern conveniences as cars and instead driving horse-drawn buggies. Amish women sometimes auction quilts to raise funds for helping poor people in other countries. Some

Violinist Joshua Bell

WORD TO KNOW

choreographers *people who design the steps for a dance performance*

Q8 ARE THERE SPECIAL ROADS FOR AMISH BUGGIES?

A8 Amish buggies share the country roads with cars. Each buggy has a big orange triangle on the back so that drivers can see it from a distance. At night, the buggies carry small battery-operated or kerosene lamps.

An Amish woman sews a quilt.

Amish stitchers sell their quilts in shops in and near Shipshewana. In barns on their farms, some Amish men make and sell wooden crafts, from simple coatracks to large pieces of furniture.

The Indiana countryside inspired its own kind of fine art painting called the Hoosier School. In the late 1800s and early 1900s, a group of Hoosier School artists painted Indiana scenes, especially in Brown County. They painted in the style of impressionism, which is more concerned with showing light and color than the details of a scene.

Hoosier sculptor Robert Indiana created an image of the word *love* in capital letters with the letter *o* tilted. This image appeared on a U.S. postage stamp in 1973 and was the first in an ongoing series of "love stamps."

MINI-BIO

LARRY BIRD: HOOSIER HOOPSTER

Calling himself the "hick from French Lick," Larry Joe Bird (1956–) went on to become one of the greatest hoop shooters in National Basketball Association (NBA) history. He was born in French Lick and attended Indiana State University, where he led the team to a 33-1 record in his senior year. He then played forward for the Boston Celtics for 13 seasons and helped the team win three NBA championships. In 1998, he was elected to the Basketball Hall of Fame. After retiring as a player, he worked as a coach and also purchased a hotel and restaurant in Terre Haute.

? **Want to know more?** See www.hoophall.com/halloffamers/bhof-larry-bird.html

High school basketball players from Columbus East and South Bend in a state championship game

BASKETBALL AND OTHER SPORTS

If Indiana had a state sport, it would be basketball. You'll find Hoosiers shooting hoops everywhere. This passion for the game even inspired a 1986 movie, *Hoosiers,* about a small-town high school basketball team in 1950s Indiana. No wonder Indiana has produced great professional players such as Oscar Robertson, Shawn Kemp, and Larry Bird. Indiana University former head coach Bobby Knight led the Hoosiers basketball team to 3 NCAA, 1 NIT, and 11 Big Ten championships. Fans also love Indiana's college football teams, especially Notre Dame's Fighting Irish, Indiana University's Hoosiers, and Purdue's Boilermakers.

78

MINI-BIO

TARA VANDERVEER: HOOSIER STAR AND WOMEN'S COACH

After playing on Indiana University's women's basketball team from 1973 to 1975, Tara VanDerveer (1953–) set off on a career that helped many young women athletes. She has coached women's basketball teams at several universities, including Stanford University. She also teaches and inspires teenage girls at her summer basketball camp in California. VanDerveer has won many honors, including places in the Women's Basketball Hall of Fame and the Indiana University Hall of Fame.

? **Want to know more?** See http://gostanford.cstv.com/sports/w-baskbl/mtt/vanderveer_tara00.html

Indiana has three professional major league sports teams. The Pacers are the men's National Basketball Association team, and the Fever are the Women's National Basketball Association team. The professional football team, the Indianapolis Colts, won the Super Bowl in 2007.

Indiana does not have a Major League Baseball team, but the state has produced some great players, such as Carl Erskine and Scott Rolen. Other Hoosier athletes

Fans welcome home the Indianapolis Colts after their Super Bowl win in 2007.

John Andretti in the 1991
Indianapolis 500

include Olympic swim champion Mark Spitz and NASCAR race drivers John Andretti, Jeff Gordon, and Tony Stewart.

Auto racing is another major sport in Indiana, with more than 50 tracks throughout the state. The Indianapolis 500, or Indy 500, draws racecar drivers from around the world to the Indianapolis Motor Speedway each year on Memorial Day. Known as "The Greatest Spectacle in Racing," the 500-mile (805 km) race consists of 200 laps around the speedway.

MINI-BIO

OSCAR ROBERTSON: THE "BIG O"

Oscar Palmer Robertson (1938–), one of the greatest athletes who ever played basketball, was born in Tennessee but grew up in Indianapolis. After college, he played for the Cincinnati Royals and the Milwaukee Bucks and was nicknamed the "Big O." He was elected to the Basketball Hall of Fame in 1979. After retiring from basketball, Robertson set up a variety of companies. In 1997, he donated a kidney to his daughter and soon after became a spokesperson for the National Kidney Foundation.

? Want to know more? See www.nba.com/history/players/robertson_summary.html

READ ABOUT

A rally for public
school funding at
the statehouse
in Indianapolis

GOVERNMENT GOVERNMENT

CHAPTER SEVEN

GOVERNMENT

★

H OW DOES INDIANA'S STATE GOVERNMENT AFFECT THE AVERAGE HOOSIER KID? Indiana's government decides how long children should stay in school and how much a family pays in taxes to keep the schools operating. It provides rules for safety at home, at school, at work, and on the highways. The courts help make sure that everyone obeys the laws.

SEE IT HERE!

THE INDIANA CAPITOL

Built in 1888, Indiana's huge capitol is laid out in the shape of a "plus" sign. The building and the grounds around it cover an area equal to two city blocks. Indiana limestone covers the exterior, and the interior is finished with marble and fine woods. A rotunda in the center of the building stretches 72 feet (22 m) across, with a ceiling made of German stained glass. Guides lead visitors' tours almost every day.

WHERE THE ACTION IS

The seat of Indiana's state government is Indianapolis, the state's second capital city. Corydon was the first state capital, from 1816 to 1825. Lawmakers started meeting in Indianapolis in 1825.

Indiana also has had two capitols. The first building was built in the 1830s. It had a poor foundation and had to be torn down in the 1860s. The next capitol had a sturdy foundation of Indiana limestone. Thrifty

Capital City

This map shows places of interest in Indianapolis, Indiana's capital city.

The capitol in Indianapolis

Hoosier lawmakers, however, wanted the new building to cost less than $2 million. When the final bills were paid in 1888, the new statehouse cost exactly $1,980,969.18.

The Indiana statehouse is one of the few state capitols that still contains all three branches of government, although more buildings have been added to house additional offices. Indiana's state government operates from a complex called Government Center, which has three main buildings—the state-

Capitol Facts

Here are some fascinating facts about Indiana's state capitol:

Dome exterior height: 234 feet (71 m)
Number of floors: 4
Length: 466 feet (142 m)
Width: 282 feet (86 m)
Dates of construction: 1880–1888

house and two office buildings called Government Center North and Government Center South.

The state government is set up according to the state constitution. Indiana has had two constitutions. The first constitution was adopted in 1816, when Indiana became a state. The state is governed by the second constitution, adopted in 1851. The constitution calls for three branches: executive, legislative, and judicial.

THE EXECUTIVE BRANCH

The governor is the elected head of Indiana's executive branch and serves a four-year term. He or she appoints the heads of departments and commissions, such as the Bureau of Motor Vehicles, and heads of governing boards, such as the Indiana University Governing Board. The governor can veto, or refuse to sign, bills. The legislature can override a veto with a simple majority vote.

The lieutenant governor takes over if the governor cannot do his or her job. The secretary of state registers businesses and oversees elections. The attorney general, the state's top lawyer, looks after the rights and safety of all Hoosiers. The auditor keeps track of the state's money. The superintendent of public instruction directs the Department of Education, which oversees the public schools.

THE LEGISLATIVE BRANCH

Passing laws that govern speed limits, taxes, and the state budget is the job of lawmakers in

WEIRD AND WACKY LAWS

Most Indiana laws make sense. They protect people or improve their lives. But some state and local laws seem downright strange. Here are a few weird laws found in Indiana:

- All black cats in French Lick have to wear bells on every Friday the 13th.
- If you put on a puppet show or a tumbling act, don't charge money for people to see it or you will be fined three dollars.
- It is illegal to take a bath at any time between the months of October and March.
- Passing a horse on the street is against the law.

Indiana State Government

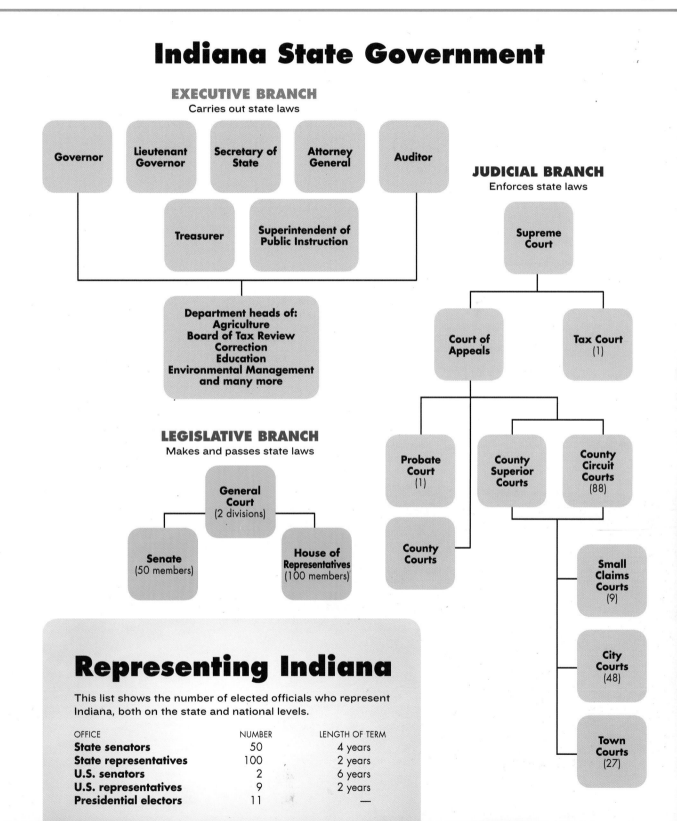

EXECUTIVE BRANCH
Carries out state laws

Governor · Lieutenant Governor · Secretary of State · Attorney General · Auditor

Treasurer · Superintendent of Public Instruction

Department heads of:
Agriculture
Board of Tax Review
Correction
Education
Environmental Management
and many more

JUDICIAL BRANCH
Enforces state laws

Supreme Court

Court of Appeals · Tax Court (1)

Probate Court (1) · County Superior Courts · County Circuit Courts (88)

County Courts

Small Claims Courts (9)

City Courts (48)

Town Courts (27)

LEGISLATIVE BRANCH
Makes and passes state laws

General Court (2 divisions)

Senate (50 members) · House of Representatives (100 members)

Representing Indiana

This list shows the number of elected officials who represent Indiana, both on the state and national levels.

OFFICE	NUMBER	LENGTH OF TERM
State senators	50	4 years
State representatives	100	2 years
U.S. senators	2	6 years
U.S. representatives	9	2 years
Presidential electors	11	—

JULIA M. CARSON: PIONEER IN CONGRESS

Julia May Carson (1938–2007) was the first woman and the first African American elected to the U.S. House of Representatives from the Indianapolis area. Born in Louisville, Kentucky, she moved with her family to Indianapolis when she was one year old. After serving in the Indiana house of representatives and the Indiana senate, she was elected to the U.S. Congress in 1996 and repeatedly won reelection. As a congresswoman, she worked to expand health insurance for children and promote veterans' rights.

? Want to know more? See http://bioguide. congress.gov/scripts/biodisplay.pl?index=C000191

the General Assembly. Indiana's General Assembly is made up of a house of representatives and a senate. A new law starts out as a bill in either the house or senate. One or more members from either house can **sponsor** the bill. A bill usually goes to one or more committees that can change it, reject it, or approve it. Once approved, the bill goes to the General Assembly for a vote.

The legislature can also suggest amendments, or changes, to the state constitution. After both houses approve an amendment, it goes to the voters. A majority of voters

The Indiana house of representatives in session

must approve the amendment before it becomes part of the constitution.

THE JUDICIAL BRANCH

Since kids are the judges and jurors of tomorrow, the Indiana Supreme Court created a project called Courts in the Classroom to help them understand Indiana's court system. Is a real-life court anything like the courts on TV? What's a **probate court**? What is the difference between a **civil** and a criminal case? Courts in the Classroom answers these and many more questions for Hoosier students in grades four through 12.

Through reenactments of historic trials, field trips to courtrooms, and Web casts and videos of trials, Hoosier kids learn that Indiana has two basic kinds of courts: trial and **appeal**.

WORDS TO KNOW

sponsor *act as a person who proposes or creates a bill*

probate court *a court that deals with wills and the property of people who have died*

civil *involving a dispute between individuals*

appeal *a legal proceeding in which a court is asked to change the decision of a lower court*

FAQ

Q8 HOW MANY CASES GO THROUGH THE INDIANA COURTS?

A8 All the courts of Indiana handle a total of more than 1.6 million cases each year.

MINI-BIO

JOHN G. ROBERTS JR.: CHIEF JUSTICE

Born in Buffalo, New York, John G. Roberts Jr. (1955–) grew up in Long Beach, Indiana, a community on the Lake Michigan shore near Michigan City. He was determined to pay his way through college and even worked in the steel mills during summers. After graduating from Harvard University in 1976, he went on to law school. He then went to Washington, D.C., where he worked for Supreme Court justices and U.S. presidents, and became a judge himself. In 2005, he became chief justice of the U.S. Supreme Court.

? Want to know more? See www.oyez. org/justices/john_g_roberts_jr/

Audience members applaud a speaker at a school board meeting in Gary.

INDIANA PRESIDENTS

William Henry Harrison (1773–1841) became the first governor in Indiana Territory in 1800 and defeated Native Americans in Indiana at the Battle of Tippecanoe in 1811. Harrison became the ninth president of the United States in 1841, but he died of pneumonia after just one month in office.

Abraham Lincoln (1809–1865) was the 16th president of the United States, serving from 1861 to 1865. Lincoln was born in Kentucky, but his family moved to Indiana in 1816, when he was seven years old. He grew up on a farm near Gentryville. He moved to Illinois at age 21. As president, he led the United States through the Civil War. He succeeded in preserving the Union but was assassinated by an angry Southerner shortly after the war ended.

Benjamin Harrison (1833–1901) was the 23rd president of the United States, serving from 1889 to 1893. The grandson of President William Henry Harrison, Benjamin Harrison was born in Ohio but lived most of his adult life in Indiana. As president, he said that the American flag must fly over all government buildings and schools.

Trial courts hear civil and criminal cases and make rulings. Indiana has four kinds of trial courts. Circuit courts are trial courts that can hold almost any kind of civil or criminal trial. Superior courts are much like circuit courts and can also act as county courts. County courts try cases involving disputes over contracts and lawsuits. They also enforce county laws. City and town courts handle traffic violations and violations of city or town laws.

Indiana Counties

This map shows the 92 counties in Indiana. Indianapolis, the state capital, is indicated with a star.

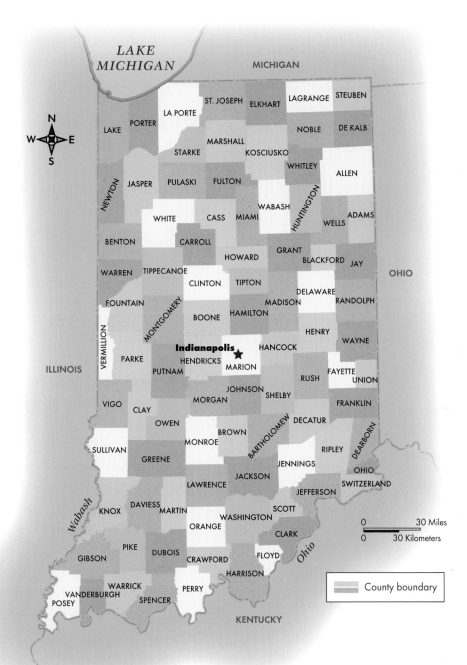

LAKE MICHIGAN

MICHIGAN

ILLINOIS

OHIO

KENTUCKY

LAKE
PORTER
LA PORTE
ST. JOSEPH
ELKHART
LAGRANGE
STEUBEN
NOBLE
DE KALB
NEWTON
STARKE
MARSHALL
KOSCIUSKO
WHITLEY
ALLEN
JASPER
PULASKI
FULTON
WABASH
HUNTINGTON
ADAMS
WHITE
CASS
MIAMI
WELLS
BENTON
CARROLL
GRANT
BLACKFORD
JAY
WARREN
TIPPECANOE
HOWARD
CLINTON
TIPTON
DELAWARE
RANDOLPH
FOUNTAIN
MADISON
MONTGOMERY
BOONE
HAMILTON
HENRY
WAYNE
VERMILLION
Indianapolis
HANCOCK
PARKE
HENDRICKS
MARION
FAYETTE
UNION
PUTNAM
RUSH
VIGO
JOHNSON
SHELBY
FRANKLIN
MORGAN
CLAY
OWEN
BARTHOLOMEW
DECATUR
BROWN
DEARBORN
SULLIVAN
MONROE
RIPLEY
GREENE
JENNINGS
OHIO
JACKSON
SWITZERLAND
LAWRENCE
JEFFERSON
Wabash
KNOX
DAVIESS
MARTIN
SCOTT
WASHINGTON
ORANGE
CLARK
Ohio
PIKE
DUBOIS
CRAWFORD
FLOYD
GIBSON
HARRISON
WARRICK
PERRY
VANDERBURGH
SPENCER
POSEY

30 Miles
30 Kilometers

County boundary

HELPING THE HISPANIC COMMUNITY

As the former director of Latino Affairs for the city of Indianapolis, Ricardo Gambetta (1964–) worked to integrate members of the fast-growing Hispanic community into Hoosier life. He was appointed the first director of this agency after Mayor Bart Peterson established it in 2000. Born in Lima, Peru, Gambetta worked as a political adviser to Peruvian government officials. He moved to Indiana in the early 1990s. He became a U.S. citizen and worked as a radio broadcaster and translator. He also helped found organizations such as Hispanic Hoosiers Inc., Indianapolis Latino Expo, and the Indiana Latino Institute.

Only New York has produced more vice presidents than Indiana's five: Schuyler Colfax (1869–1873), Thomas A. Hendricks (1885), Charles W. Fairbanks (1905–1909), Thomas Riley Marshall (1913–1921), and Dan Quayle (1989–1993).

Appellate courts reconsider cases that have already been decided. The court of appeals and the tax court both review earlier cases. From there, any appeal goes to the Indiana Supreme Court, the state's highest court.

LOCAL GOVERNMENT

Indiana has more than 3,000 local governments set up at county, township, city, town, and school district levels. The local governments have a lot to say about how Hoosiers govern themselves. Indiana lawmakers in 1980 made Indiana a "home rule" state. This means that local officials, rather than any other officials, have the power to make decisions that they think are in the best interest of their city or town.

Indiana has 92 counties, and each county is governed by a council and a board of commissioners. The council passes property and other taxes, sets county salaries, and pays the county's bills. The commissioners look after county roads and other property, appoint most county officials, and enact laws and rules involving matters such as housing and traffic control. Counties are divided into 1,008 rural or urban townships governed by a trustee and three board members, all elected to four-year terms.

Cities are governed by a mayor and city council. Towns are governed by a town council, which elects a council president. Cities and towns are responsible for police and fire protection, local parks, streets, water pipes, sewers, and building safety.

Indianapolis and surrounding Marion County have a special type of local government. The city and the county merged as of 1970 to operate as the City of Indianapolis.

Indiana's school district governments can pass some taxes and borrow money to operate the public schools. An elected or appointed school board or a board of trustees governs each school district.

These police officers in Indianapolis are some of the many government workers who serve the state.

State Flag

Indiana's state flag features a flaming golden torch and golden stars against a field of blue. The torch stands for liberty and enlightenment, whose effects are shown in the golden rays that stream from the torch. The outer circle of 13 stars stands for the 13 original states. The five stars of the inner arc represent the next five states to enter the Union. Indiana, the 19th state, is the large star directly above the flame, with the word *Indiana* in a half circle above it. The General Assembly adopted this design in 1917 as part of Indiana's 1916 centennial celebration.

State Seal

The state seal shows three hills in the center, with trees on either side. The sun is setting behind the hills, with 14 rays coming out—13 rays for the original colonies and the 14th representing Indiana. On the right is a woodsman with an axe, and a buffalo jumping over a log is to the left. On the ground are shoots of bluegrass. Above the center are the words "Seal of the State of Indiana," and underneath is 1816—the year of Indiana's statehood. On each side of the date is a diamond with dots on both sides and leaves of the tulip tree, the state tree. The state seal was adopted in 1963.

READ ABOUT

A worker on
an automobile
assembly line
in Princeton

CHAPTER EIGHT

ECONOMY

★

WHEN YOU SEE A MOTOR HOME, TRAILER TRUCK, OR RECREATIONAL VEHICLE ON THE HIGHWAY, THERE IS A GOOD CHANCE IT WAS MADE IN INDIANA. The Hoosier State is a leading maker of all kinds of transportation equipment. Indiana also produces tons of corn and piles of coal. In addition, Indiana is a leading maker of pharmaceutical drugs and medical equipment.

A farmer plows an Indiana field.

INDIANA'S GOOD EARTH

Even though few people work on farms, Indiana's rich prairie soil plays a big role in the Hoosier economy. More than 65 percent of Indiana's land is still used for farming. Indiana is the third-largest among the states in growing soybeans—almost 200 million bushels in 2007. Indiana ranks among the top five states in corn production with more than 1 billion bushels in 2007. Indiana is second only to California in producing tomatoes for processing into ketchup and canned goods. Hogs and chickens are the top livestock products for the Hoosier State.

Top Products

Agriculture crops Corn, soybeans, tomatoes
Agriculture livestock Hogs, cattle, dairy products, chickens
Manufacturing Transportation equipment, truck bodies, motor homes, steel, aluminum
Mining Coal, limestone, sand and gravel, clays, gypsum

Major Agricultural and Mining Products

This map shows where Indiana's major agricultural and mining products come from. See a cow? That means cattle are raised there.

Cattle
Chemicals
Coal
Dairy
Fruit
Grains
Hay
Hogs
Manufacturing
Melons

Mineral mining
Natural gas
Oats
Oil
Potatoes
Poultry
Sheep
Soybeans
Tobacco
Vegetables

Urban area
Forests, some farming
Farming

A dairy cow on a milking machine in Zionsville

WORDS TO KNOW

biofuels *energy sources made from plants or plant-derived materials*

biodiesel *fuel made from soybeans and diesel oil*

Indiana is a leading producer of processed dairy products. Only California makes more ice cream than Indiana. Hoosier corn mills produce much of the corn syrup used in making soft drinks.

Biofuels are made from agricultural products. Some Indiana corn is used to produce ethanol, an alcohol that is blended with gasoline to make cleaner-burning fuel for cars. At the end of 2006, about 38 million bushels out of more than 900 million bushels of Indiana corn were used to make about 102 million gallons (386 million liters) of ethanol. Researchers at Purdue University estimate that new processing plants being built in Indiana in 2007 will eventually use about 203 million bushels of Indiana's annual corn crop.

Indiana's soybean crop is being used to make **biodiesel**. The world's largest biodiesel fuel plant opened in Claypool in August 2007. It is able to process 50 million bushels of Indiana soybeans every year.

Miners take about 35 million tons of coal a year from deposits found in southern Indiana. The coal, however, contains a lot of sulfur and causes air pollution. New technology for burning coal with less pollution allows some Indiana coal to be used as a fuel for electric power plants.

Indiana limestone is used in the construction industry. More than 220 million tons of limestone blocks are cut from Indiana quarries each year. The state's quarries also produce about 60 millions tons of crushed limestone and more than 30 million tons of sand and gravel every year.

The National Cathedral in Washington, D.C., is built mainly of Indiana limestone, and it is one of the materials on the exterior of the Empire State Building in New York City.

HOOSIER-MADE GOODS

Many jobs in factories and steel mills have disappeared since the 1980s. Some of these jobs have moved to foreign countries. Still, manufacturing plays a bigger role in Indiana's economy than it does in many other states.

Indiana's number-one industry is making transportation equipment. Thousands of railroad cars, truck and bus bodies, motor homes, auto parts, and airplane parts roll off of Hoosier assembly lines. Indiana also makes huge amounts of iron, steel, and chemicals. Indiana's chemical industry centers on drug manufacturing.

MINI-BIO

ELI LILLY: DRUG COMPANY FOUNDER

Eli Lilly (1838–1898) founded in Indianapolis what became one of the world's largest drug companies. Born in Maryland, Lilly moved with his family to Indiana. After serving as a Union army colonel during the Civil War, he set up a company in Indianapolis to make high-quality medicines that could be given only through doctors. Eventually, his son and grandsons took over the business. They built it into Eli Lilly & Company.

? Want to know more? See www.lilly.com/about/history.html

Q8 WHAT IS THE BIGGEST COMPANY IN INDIANA?

A8 As of 2007, Berry Plastics Corporation of Evansville is Indiana's biggest company, with 6,900 employees in Indiana and elsewhere and revenues of $3.1 billion.

MOTOR SPORTS INDUSTRY

Racing is more than just a sport in Indiana. Events at the Indianapolis Motor Speedway bring tourists as well as race teams to Indianapolis. From 2000 to 2007, three races—the Indianapolis 500, the Brickyard 400, and the United States Grand Prix—added an estimated $727 million each year to the economy of Indianapolis.

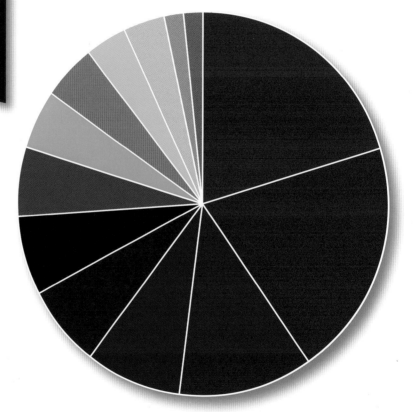

What Do Hoosiers Do?

This color-coded chart shows what industries Hoosiers work in.

- **20.4%** Manufacturing, 597,542
- **20.1%** Educational services, health care, and social assistance, 590,392
- **11.5%** Retail trade, 336,396
- **8.4%** Arts, entertainment, recreation, accommodation, and food services, 244,588
- **6.9%** Construction, 200,677
- **6.7%** Professional, scientific, administrative, and waste management services, 195,577
- **5.9%** Finance, insurance, real estate, rental, and leasing, 171,635
- **5.1%** Transportation, warehousing, and utilities, 148,538
- **4.7%** Other services, except public administration, 136,796
- **3.5%** Wholesale trade, 101,210
- **3.5%** Public administration, 100,979
- **1.9%** Information, 54,293
- **1.4%** Agriculture, forestry, fishing, hunting, and mining, 39,430

Source: U.S. Census Bureau, 2005

HOOSIERS AT YOUR SERVICE

What do teachers, doctors, hairstylists, and pizza delivery people have in common? They are all service industry workers. Like many other states, the service industry plays a big role in Indiana's economy. Wholesale and retail sales are the top service industries. The service industry is the fastest-growing part of Indiana's economy. During the 1990s, service industry jobs grew by 40 percent. About 25 percent of all Hoosier workers hold jobs in the service industry.

Hoosiers are also looking to become leaders in new industries. One such industry is called logistics. Workers in the logistics industry use computers and other high-tech equipment to schedule shipments. They help transport goods from manufacturers to consumers quickly and at the lowest cost. Joanne Joyce, president and chief executive of the Indianapolis Private Industry Council, believes in helping young people acquire the skills they need to do these new jobs. "Central Indiana is the crossroads of America," she says, "and . . . we are ready to forge ahead as the crossroads of innovation and information."

This jewelry salesclerk is one of the many service workers in Indiana.

LAKE MICHIGAN

MICHIGAN

94

Michigan City
Porter
South Bend
Bristol

80 90

Hammond
Gary
La Porte
Elkhart
Goshen
Shipshewana
Angola

Schererville
Valparaiso
Nappanee
Auburn

Crown Point
Plymouth
Winona Lake
Maumee

Lowell
Kankakee
Warsaw
North
Fort Wayne
469

Medaryville
Rochester
Manchester

Rensselaer
Huntington
Decatur

Monticello
Logansport
Peru
Bluffton

Wabash
Marion
69
Geneva

West
Lafayette
Kokomo
OHIO

Lafayette
Hartford City
Portland

Frankfort
Elwood

74
Lebanon
Noblesville
Anderson
Muncie

Crawfordsville
Fishers
Winchester

Geographic
Center of Indiana
465
Fountain City

Dana
Brownsburg
Greenfield
Richmond
70

ILLINOIS
Plainfield
Indianapolis
Cambridge City
Connersville

Terre
Haute
70
Greenwood
74
Shelbyville

Martinsville
Franklin
Metamora

Greensburg

Nashville
Columbus
Batesville

Bloomington
65
North Vernon

W. Fk. White
Seymour

E. Fk. White
Madison

Vincennes
Mitchell
Salem

West Baden Springs
French Lick
Ohio

Jasper
Marengo
265

Wabash
Leavenworth
New Albany

64
Lincoln
City
Corydon

164
Santa Claus

Evansville

Mt. Vernon
Rockport

KENTUCKY

Ohio

N
W   E
S

0   40 Miles

0   40 Kilometers

70   Interstate highway

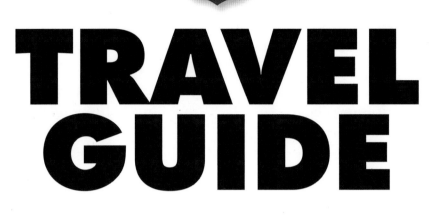

CHAPTER NINE

TRAVEL GUIDE

TRAVEL GUIDE

★

FROM THE STUNNING SHORES OF LAKE MICHIGAN TO THE CAVES AND ROCK FORMATIONS NEAR THE OHIO RIVER, INDIANA IS A LAND OF STUNNING NATURAL BEAUTY. On a trip through Indiana, you can visit the state's fields and plains, hike its trails, observe its wildlife, and walk in the footsteps of people who lived long ago.

← Follow along with this travel map. We'll begin in Auburn and travel all the way to Vincennes.

NORTHERN

THINGS TO DO: Check out antique cars, shop for quilts, and scramble up a sand dune.

Auburn

★ **Auburn Cord Duesenberg Automobile Museum:** You'll see many fine automobiles produced in Indiana in the early 1900s and discover how the Indiana auto industry evolved from horse-drawn carriages to horseless carriages to full-scale automobile production.

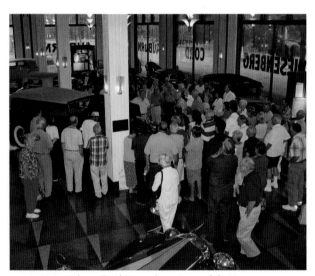

Auburn Cord Duesenberg Automobile Museum

Bristol

★ **Bonneyville Mill:** Watch big belts moving and hear wheels creaking as water from the millpond turns the machinery that operates this 150-year-old gristmill. Bags of flour and cornmeal are for sale in the miller's shop.

Elkhart

★ **National New York Central Railroad Museum:** At this museum, you can learn about some of the railroad history that helped make Indiana the "Crossroads of America." Indoor and outdoor exhibits include videos, interactive displays, model railroads, and actual locomotives and railcars.

LaPorte

★ **LaPorte County Fair:** Indiana's oldest county fair is held every July at the LaPorte County Fairgrounds. You can view prize-winning animals, watch a horse race, and enjoy rides and other attractions at this authentic Hoosier experience.

Goshen

★ **Michiana Mennonite Relief Sale:** The centerpiece of this event, held at the Elkhart County Fairgrounds each September, is the Amish quilt auction. Start the day with a breakfast of pancakes and sausage, and stop by the antique auction and displays of crafts made all over the world.

★ **Hesston Steam Museum:** If it took a steam engine to run it, you will probably find it here. This outdoor museum of machines contains steam-driven devices of all kinds, including a locomotive, a sawmill, a steam crane, and a power plant. Taking a ride on a miniature train hauled by a miniature locomotive is fun for kids of all ages.

Medaryville

★ **Jasper-Pulaski State Fish & Wildlife Area:** Every autumn, this wildlife area fills with up to 15,000 greater sandhill cranes. The cranes stop off there on the way from their summer homes in Canada and northern states to Florida.

Michigan City

★ **Ragtops Museum:** More than 65 convertibles are on display at this auto museum. You can also step into reproductions of a service station and a rock-and-roll diner from the 1950s. The diner exhibit includes antique jukeboxes and pinball machines.

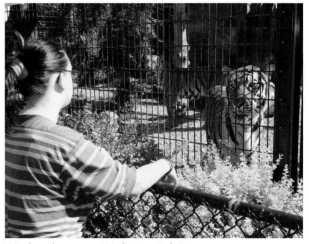

Watching the tigers at Washington Park Zoo

★ **Washington Park Zoo:** Lions, tigers, bears, alligators, boa constrictors, geckos, baboons, and mangabeys—along with more than 200 other animals—can be found at this zoo on the Lake Michigan dunes.

Nappanee

★ **Amish Acres Historic Farm and Heritage Resort:** In a parklike setting, you can take a tour of an Amish farmhouse built in 1893, a round barn and other outbuildings, and a garden. Then ride a farm wagon around the grounds and see demonstrations of crafts such as quilting and candle making. At the Restaurant Barn, enjoy a family-style dinner with Amish favorites such as beef and noodles.

Peru

★ **Grissom Air Museum:** Visit this aviation museum and state historic site to see and touch warplanes that made history from World War II through the Gulf War. The museum is named in honor of astronaut Virgil "Gus" Grissom.

Porter

★ **Indiana Dunes National Lakeshore:** This is the only national lakeshore in the United States. Learn all about dunes at the Calumet Dune Interpretive Center, hike miles of scenic trails, climb a dune, watch birds, or take a swim in Lake Michigan.

★ **Splash Down Dunes Water Park:** If swimming in Lake Michigan at the Indiana Dunes isn't exciting enough for you, travel inland and experience the attractions at this water park.

Shipshewana

★ **Menno-Hof Amish/Mennonite Interpretive Center:** Learn about the Amish and Mennonite groups that live in this area of Indiana. You may enjoy looking at crafts in the town's shops and trying hearty Amish foods at the bakeries and restaurants.

South Bend

★ **South Bend Chocolate Factory and Museum:** Who doesn't like creamy chocolate candy? See how these treats are made and learn about the history of chocolate on a tour of this candy factory. Then finish off your visit with some free candy samples.

SEE IT HERE!

COLLEGE FOOTBALL HALL OF FAME

Review video footage of historic football games, sit in a replica of a press box, and test your own football skills at this museum in South Bend dedicated to student athletes. You can also see exhibits honoring winners of the Heisman and MacArthur Bowl trophies.

College Football Hall of Fame

★ **Studebaker National Museum:** Learn about the history of Hoosier automobiles made from 1904 to 1966. Not only does the museum contain examples of Studebaker models, it also displays other fine cars once made in Indiana, as well as some horse-drawn carriages, including one used by President Abraham Lincoln.

Topeka

★ **Hoosier Buggy Shop:** Who makes horse-drawn carriages and buggies these days? The answer is the Hochstetler brothers in their Hoosier Buggy Shop. Take a tour to see how they are made.

Visitors at the Taltree Arboretum & Gardens

Valparaiso

★ **Taltree Arboretum & Gardens:** This retreat from urban life includes gardens, wetlands, woodlands, and prairies containing many varieties of prairie wildflowers, as well as thousands of oak and hickory trees.

Winona Lake

★ **Village at Winona:** You can attend concerts and festivals and shop for artwork in this restored village along the shore of Winona Lake. The area was developed in the early 1900s as a summer retreat and conference grounds for several religious groups. You can tour the home of evangelist Billy Sunday, mentioned in the song "Chicago."

Studebaker National Museum

A visitor and sea lion at the Fort Wayne Children's Zoo

Fort Wayne

★ **Fort Wayne Children's Zoo:** Find penguins, monkeys, sea lions, and other creatures at this acclaimed children's zoo. See kangaroos, echidnas, sharks, and rays at Australian Adventure. Take a walk through the Indonesian Rainforest and pay a visit to the Komodo dragon. There are also pony rides, a dugout canoe ride, the Sky Safari, the Zoo Train, and an endangered species carousel.

★ **Foellinger-Freimann Botanical Conservatory:** These gardens are right in downtown Fort Wayne. The botanical conservatory has three indoor gardens and four outdoor gardens containing some 1,200 plants. The indoor Showcase Garden displays change with the seasons.

Monticello

★ **Indiana Beach Amusement Resort:** Hang on as you ride on five roller coasters and enjoy more than 20 other rides and attractions. The amusement park also contains a water park and swimming beach on Lake Shafer. You can even relax with a ride on the *Shafer Queen*, a paddle-wheel riverboat.

Indiana Beach Amusement Resort

CENTRAL

THINGS TO DO: Relive auto racing thrills, step back in time to a pioneer town, and admire great Native American art.

Cambridge City

★ **Huddleston Farmhouse:** See this spot where pioneers traveling the National Road to new homes in the West stopped to rest. Tour the house, barn, and other buildings on the grounds to learn about the daily lives of early Hoosier settlers.

Making pottery at the Conner Prairie Living History Museum

Fishers

★ **Conner Prairie Living History Museum:** Costumed guides take you on a tour of historic areas on this site near Indianapolis. You can see how French fur traders and Native Americans lived, visit a Victorian farmhouse, explore a pioneer village, and much more.

Geneva

★ **Limberlost:** This home in Adams County belonged to nature photographer and writer Gene (Geneva) Stratton-Porter. The area was once a swampland called Limberlost.

Dana

★ **Ernie Pyle State Historic Site:** The farmhouse where World War II correspondent Ernie Pyle was

ERNIE PYLE: COURAGEOUS CORRESPONDENT

Reporter Ernest Taylor Pyle (1900–1945) was born on a farm near Dana. He traveled with U.S. troops during World War II to battlefields in Africa, Europe, and the South Pacific. People back home eagerly read his accounts of how the soldiers lived and fought. Pyle was killed by Japanese gunfire during the Battle of Okinawa.

? Want to know more? See www.in.gov/ism/StateHistoricSites/ErniePyleHome/ep_histsig.aspx

born is now a museum. Exhibits tell about his career and his role in reporting from battlefields during World War II.

Indianapolis

★ **Eiteljorg Museum of American Indians and Western Art:** This is the only museum in the Midwest showing both Native American and American Western artwork. It contains works by traditional and contemporary artists, including N. C. Wyeth, Andy Warhol, Georgia O'Keeffe, Frederic Remington, and Kay WalkingStick.

★ **President Benjamin Harrison Home:** The home where President Harrison once lived is now a library and museum. You can walk through 10 of the rooms in the large house and see how they were furnished when Harrison lived here.

★ **Indiana Historical Society:** The historical society contains a vast amount of information about Indiana's history and people. The collections include 33,000 digital images, 5,000 manuscript collections, 14,000 pieces of sheet music, and 1.6 million photographs. This is a great place to find primary sources.

★ **Indianapolis Motor Speedway Hall of Fame Museum:** This museum contains a collection of antique and racing cars, including more than 30 of the cars that have won the Indy 500. In a theater at the museum, you can watch a film about this classic auto race held almost every Memorial Day since 1911. The race was not held during the years of World War I or World War II.

SEE IT HERE!

CHILDREN'S MUSEUM OF INDIANAPOLIS

Hands-on exhibits bring learning to life. The "All Aboard..." exhibit celebrates the history of Indiana's railroads. Dinosphere takes visitors back 65 million years. Passport to the World introduces kids to other lands and cultures. In addition, there are changing events and activities throughout the year.

Metamora

★ **Whitewater Canal State Historic Site:** Take a 25-minute cruise on the *Ben Franklin III*, a canal boat pulled by a horse. Your ride is along one of the few Indiana canals that were built before the coming of the railroads.

FAQ

Q8 HAVE WOMEN EVER COMPETED IN THE INDY 500?

A8 Yes, four women drivers competed in the race between 1977 and 2006. The first woman racer was Janet Guthrie.

Marion

★ **Quilters Hall of Fame:**
Established in the home of quilter
Marie Webster, the Hall of Fame
hosts changing exhibits of hand-
made quilts, representing a variety
of themes, throughout the year.

Fountain City

★ **Levi Coffin House State Historic
Site:** Imagine the danger of escap-
ing from slavery using wagons with
false bottoms and safe houses with
hidden doors. You can see all this
and more at the redbrick home of
Levi Coffin and his wife, Catharine.
It was one of the stops on the
Underground Railroad.

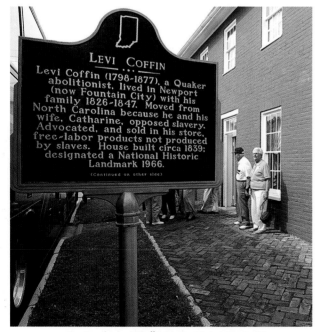

Touring the Levi Coffin House State Historic Site

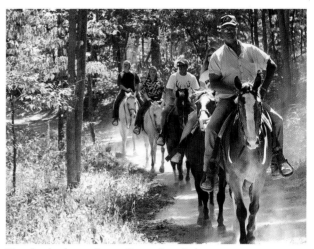

Horseback riding at Brown County State Park

Nashville

★ **Brown County State Park:**
Covering 16,000 acres (6,500 ha),
this is Indiana's largest state park.
About 1.5 million visitors come
each year for pleasures such as a
self-guided walking tour around
the park's Ogle Hollow Nature
Preserve. There are 70 miles (113
km) of horseback riding trails and
12 miles (19 km) of steep, rugged
hiking trails.

★ **T. C. Steele State Historic Site:**
Tour the home where Hoosier
School painter Theodore Clement
Steele created his art in the early
1900s. In the studio, you can see
exhibits of his work. He often
painted scenes around this Brown
County summer home, which he
called "the House of the Singing
Winds."

Crawfordsville

★ **Turkey Run State Park:** Some of southern Indiana's most beautiful scenery lies inside the borders of this state park near Crawfordsville and along Sugar Creek. You can hike or horseback ride along the park's miles of trails that go through ancient forest. You can also rent a cabin on the grounds and stay the night.

Kayakers at Turkey Run State Park

SOUTHERN

THINGS TO DO: Hike rugged trails, wander through spectacular caves, or take a ride on an old-fashioned train.

Corydon

★ **Battle of Corydon Memorial Park:** This 5-acre (2 ha) state park was the site of Indiana's only Civil War battle. It is where the Harrison County Home Guard tried but failed to stop General John Hunt Morgan's Confederate troops after they crossed the Ohio River from Kentucky into Indiana. You can follow the route taken by Morgan from Corydon along the John Hunt Morgan Heritage Trail.

★ **Corydon State Capitol:** Indiana's first capitol was this square, limestone building built in the early 1800s. Hoosier lawmakers met here from 1816 to 1825. Exhibits inside tell about Indiana's early history.

French Lick-West Baden Springs

★ **Indiana Railway Museum:** See steam, electric, and diesel locomotives at this museum dedicated to Hoosier railroad history. The museum also has a large collection of antique passenger cars, freight cars, and cabooses. The highlight of a visit, however, is a two-hour ride aboard an old train along parts of the Hoosier National Forest and through a 2,200-foot (670 m) tunnel.

★ **West Baden Springs Hotel:** The mineral springs in this area have been popular since the late 1770s, when George Rogers Clark is said to have discovered them. Many people claimed that the mineral waters cured them of all kinds of diseases. They came to stay at hotels like the West Baden Springs Hotel. The historic hotel was restored and reopened in the early 2000s.

SEE IT HERE!

LISTEN TO THIS

Have you ever heard of a Calliola, a Decap, or a Limonaire? They are all fantastically odd musical instruments that you will find at an unusual museum in Dale called Dr. Ted's Musical Marvels. The biggest instrument in the collection is a Wurlitzer organ made for carousels in the early 1900s.

Jasper

★ **Dubois County Museum:** One of the largest county museums in Indiana is dedicated to the German immigrants who settled the area in the 1800s. Among the many exhibits are a log cabin and a ship's bunk like the ones immigrants squeezed into on the trip across the Atlantic Ocean.

Leavenworth

★ **Wyandotte Caves:** Take a guided tour through these beautiful limestone caves under the Harrison-Crawford State Forest. You will learn about the geology of Indiana that gave rise to huge underground rooms and fantastic rock formations.

Exploring Wyandotte Caves

Lincoln Boyhood National Memorial

Lincoln City

★ **Lincoln Boyhood National Memorial:** Walk the land where Abraham Lincoln spent his boyhood years from ages seven to 21. The site contains memorials to Lincoln and to his mother, Nancy, who is buried there. A museum tells about the boyhood life of Lincoln.

Madison

★ **Lanier Mansion State Historic Site:** This mansion was once the home of James Franklin Doughty Lanier, who helped bring railroads into Indiana. You can tour the house, stroll in the gardens, and learn about Lanier's contributions to the growth of Indiana.

Marengo

★ **Marengo Cave National Landmark:** See giant **stalactites** hanging from the ceiling of this spectacular cave, the only national landmark among the many caves in southern Indiana. You can admire an underground waterfall, walk through a "room" of lovely mineral crystals, and even pan for gemstones.

WORD TO KNOW

stalactites *columns or pillars formed on the ceiling of a cave from dripping groundwater*

Mitchell

★ **Spring Mill State Park:** History, hiking, and a whole lot more await visitors to this Indiana state park. You will find underground adventure in the park's Twin Caves, history at the Pioneer Village and Gristmill, and wildlife facts at the Nature Center.

Grinding corn at Spring Mill State Park

New Albany

★ **Culbertson Mansion:** Find out how the rich lived way back when. One of Indiana's wealthiest businessmen, William S. Culbertson, built this 25-room mansion in 1867. The mansion features hand-painted ceilings, marble fireplaces, and a carved rosewood staircase.

SEE IT HERE!

SKI SOUTHERN INDIANA?

Whether or not there is snow, Hoosiers can gather at Paoli Peaks for winter fun. Snowmaking equipment pumps the white flakes onto the 300-foot-high (90 m) natural hill. The slopes can hold more than 11,000 skiers or snowboarders per hour.

Rockport

★ **Lincoln Pioneer Village and Museum:** Set in a grassy park are log cabins, log houses, schools, churches, and other buildings that look just as they did when Abe Lincoln lived in Spencer County. Visit the museum to see items used in everyday life on the Hoosier frontier.

Santa Claus

★ **Holiday World & Splashin' Safari:** Yes, there is a Santa Claus, Indiana. It is home to a 100-acre (40 ha) theme park that features thrill rides, kids' rides, live shows, and a water park. Where did the town name come from? According to local legend, the German founders meeting at a church were searching for a suitable town name on Christmas Eve 1852. The wind blew the church doors open, and the people heard sleigh bells ringing outside. The children cried, "It's Santa Claus!"

Vincennes

★ **Vincennes State Historic Sites:** To get a feel for what life was like in old Vincennes, head for Harrison Street and the historic buildings preserved or reproduced there. Start with an orientation at the Log Cabin Visitors Center. Next door is the "Red House," the name lawmakers of Indiana Territory gave to their meeting place when Vincennes was the territorial capital. Then stop by the replica of the Elihu Stout Print Shop, where the laws of the territory, as well as its first newspaper, were printed.

SCIENCE, TECHNOLOGY, & MATH PROJECTS

Make weather maps, graph population statistics, and research endangered species that live in the state.

120

PRIMARY VS. SECONDARY SOURCES

121

So what are primary and secondary sources? And what's the diff? This section explains all that and where you can find them.

BIOGRAPHICAL DICTIONARY

133

This at-a-glance guide highlights some of the state's most important and influential people. Visit this section and read about their contributions to the state, the country, and the world.

RESOURCES

Books, Web sites, DVDs, and more. Take a look at these additional sources for information about the state.

137

WRITING PROJECTS

★ ★ ★

Write a Memoir, Journal, or Editorial for Your School Newspaper!

Picture Yourself . . .

★ in a Mississippian home. What types of skills would you be learning? What would your responsibilities be? What kinds of crops would you be growing? How would life be different from the way your life is today?

SEE: Chapter Two, pages 29–30.
GO TO: www.in.gov/ism/StateHistoricSites/AngelMounds/am_histsig.aspx

★ at Fort Ouiatenon. What types of people would you see there? What would people be doing, and why would they be bustling around?

SEE: Chapter Three, pages 36–37.
GO TO: www.tcha.mus.in.us/materials.htm

Create an Election Brochure or Web Site!

Run for office! Throughout this book, you've read about some of the issues that concern Indiana today. As a candidate for governor of Indiana, create a campaign brochure or Web site.

★ Explain how you meet the qualifications to be governor of Indiana.

★ Talk about the three or four major issues you'll focus on if you're elected.

★ Remember, you'll be responsible for Indiana's budget. How would you spend the taxpayers' money?

SEE: Chapter Seven, pages 84–85.

GO TO: The Indiana government Web site at www.in.gov. You may also want to read some local newspapers. Try these:
Indianapolis Star at www.indystar.com
Fort Wayne Journal Gazette at www.journalgazette.net
Evansville Courier & Press at www.courierpress.com

Create an interview script with a Hoosier!

★ Research various Hoosiers, such as Larry Bird, John G. Roberts Jr., Richard G. Hatcher, Madame C. J. Walker, Oscar Robertson, or Jane Pauley.

★ Based on your research, pick one person you would most like to talk with.

★ Write a script of the interview. What questions would you ask? How would this person answer? Create a question-and-answer format. You may want to supplement this writing project with a voice-recording dramatization of the interview.

SEE: Chapters Five, Six, and Seven, pages 56–91, and the Biographical Dictionary, pages 133–136.

GO TO: www.indianahistory.org/Library/notable.html

ART PROJECTS

★ ★ ★

Create a PowerPoint Presentation or Visitors' Guide

Welcome to Indiana!

Indiana is a great place to visit and to live! From its natural beauty to its bustling cities and historical sites, there's plenty to see and do. In your PowerPoint presentation or brochure, highlight 10 to 15 of Indiana's amazing landmarks. Be sure to include:

★ a map of the state showing where these sites are located

★ photos, illustrations, Web links, natural history facts, geographic stats, climate and weather, plants and wildlife, and recent discoveries

SEE: Chapters One and Nine, pages 8–23 and 102–115, and Fast Facts, pages 126–127.

GO TO: The official tourism Web site for Indiana at www.visitindiana.com. Download and print maps, photos, and vacation ideas for tourists.

Illustrate the Lyrics to the Indiana State Song

("On the Banks of the Wabash, Far Away")

Use markers, paints, photos, collages, colored pencils, or computer graphics to illustrate the lyrics to "On the Banks of the Wabash, Far Away." Turn your illustrations into a picture book, or scan them into PowerPoint and add music.

SEE: The lyrics to "On the Banks of the Wabash, Far Away" on page 128.

GO TO: The Indiana state government Web site at www.in.gov to find out more about the origin of the state song.

State Quarter Project

From 1999 to 2008, the U.S. Mint introduced new quarters commemorating each of the 50 states in the order that they were admitted to the Union. Each state's quarter features a unique design on its back, or reverse.

GO TO: www.usmint.gov/kids and find out what's featured on the back of the Indiana quarter.

★ Research the significance of the image. Who designed the quarter? Who chose the final design?

★ Design your own Indiana quarter. What images would you choose for the reverse?

★ Make a poster showing the Indiana quarter and label each image.

SCIENCE, TECHNOLOGY, & MATH PROJECTS

★ ★ ★

Graph Population Statistics!

★ Compare population statistics (such as ethnic background, birth, death, and literacy rates) in Indiana counties or major cities.

★ In your graph or chart, look at population density and write sentences describing what the population statistics show; graph one set of population statistics and write a paragraph explaining what the graphs reveal.

SEE: Chapter Six, pages 66–79.

GO TO: Check out the official Web site for the U.S. Census Bureau at www.census.gov and at http://quickfacts.census.gov/qfd/states/18000.html to find out more about population statistics, how they work, and what the statistics are for Indiana.

Create a Weather Map of Indiana!

Use your knowledge of Indiana's geography to research and identify conditions that result in specific weather events. What is it about the geography of Indiana that makes it vulnerable to things such as tornadoes? Create a weather map or poster that shows the weather patterns across the state. To accompany your map, explain the technology used to measure weather phenomena and provide data.

SEE: Chapter One, pages 8–23.

GO TO: The National Oceanic and Atmospheric Administration's National Weather Service Web site at www.weather.gov for weather maps and forecasts for Indiana.

Karner blue butterfly

Track Endangered Species

Using your knowledge of Indiana's wildlife, research what animals and plants are endangered or threatened.

★ Find out what the state is doing to protect these species.

★ Chart known populations of the animals and plants, and report on changes in certain geographic areas.

SEE: Chapter One, pages 16–23.

GO TO: Web sites such as www.in.gov/dnr/fishwild/endangered/e-list.htm for lists of endangered species in Indiana.

PRIMARY VS. SECONDARY SOURCES

★ ★ ★

What's the Diff?

Your teacher may require at least one or two primary sources and one or two secondary sources for your assignment. So, what's the difference between the two?

★ **Primary sources are original.** You are reading the actual words of someone's diary, journal, letter, autobiography, or interview. Primary sources can also be photographs, maps, prints, cartoons, news/film footage, posters, first-person newspaper articles, drawings, musical scores, and recordings. By the way, when you conduct a survey, interview someone, shoot a video, or take photographs to include in a project, you are creating primary sources!

★ **Secondary sources are what you find in encyclopedias, textbooks, articles, biographies, and almanacs.** These are written by a person or group of people who tell about something that happened to someone else. Secondary sources also recount what another person said or did. This book is an example of a secondary source.

Now that you know what primary sources are—where can you find them?

★ **Your school or local library:** Check the library catalog for collections of original writings, government documents, musical scores, and so on. Some of this material may be stored on microfilm. The Library of Congress Web site (www.loc.gov) is an excellent online resource for primary source materials.

★ **Historical societies:** These organizations keep historical documents, photographs, and other materials. Staff members can help you find what you are looking for. History museums are also great places to see primary sources firsthand.

★ **The Internet:** There are lots of sites that have primary sources you can download and use in a project or assignment.

TIMELINE

★ ★ ★

U.S. Events   BCE   **Indiana Events**

1400

c. 10,000 BCE
The first people arrive in Indiana.

1492
Christopher Columbus and his crew sight land in the Caribbean Sea.

1450 CE
Mississippian people abandon their city at Angel Mounds.

1600

1607
The first permanent English settlement in North America is established at Jamestown.

René Robert Cavelier, Sieur de La Salle

1620
Pilgrims found Plymouth Colony, the second permanent English settlement.

1679
René-Robert Cavelier, Sieur de La Salle, explores northern Indiana, claiming it for France.

1700

1732
The French found Vincennes, Indiana's first permanent European settlement.

1763
The British take over New France at the end of the French and Indian War.

1776
Thirteen American colonies declare their independence from Great Britain.

1779
George Rogers Clark recaptures Fort Sackville from British forces.

1783
The United States wins British land that becomes the Northwest Territory.

1787
The U.S. Constitution is written.

1795
The Treaty of Greenville gives lands in the Northwest Territory to Native Americans.

U.S. Events `1800` **Indiana Events**

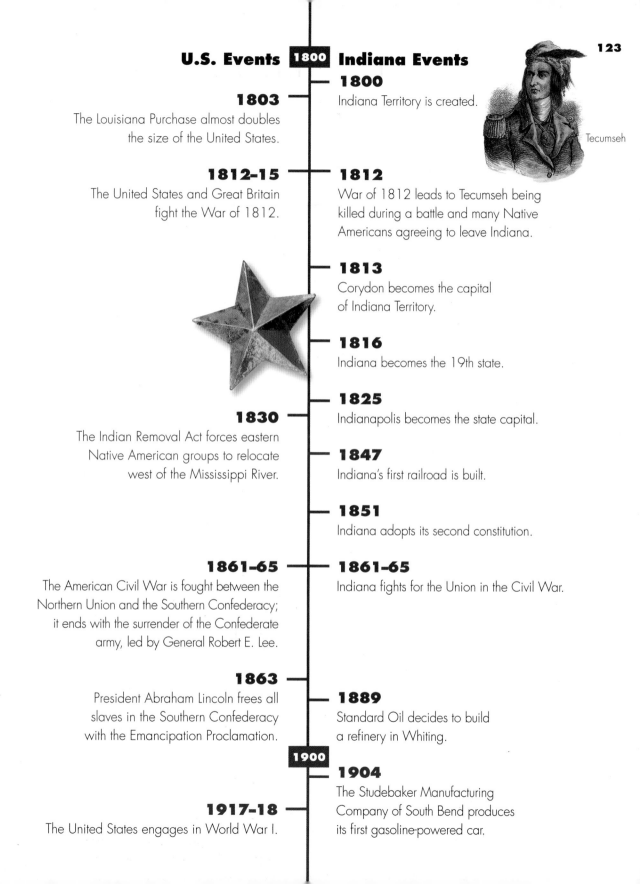

Tecumseh

1800
Indiana Territory is created.

1803
The Louisiana Purchase almost doubles the size of the United States.

1812–15
The United States and Great Britain fight the War of 1812.

1812
War of 1812 leads to Tecumseh being killed during a battle and many Native Americans agreeing to leave Indiana.

1813
Corydon becomes the capital of Indiana Territory.

1816
Indiana becomes the 19th state.

1825
Indianapolis becomes the state capital.

1830
The Indian Removal Act forces eastern Native American groups to relocate west of the Mississippi River.

1847
Indiana's first railroad is built.

1851
Indiana adopts its second constitution.

1861–65
The American Civil War is fought between the Northern Union and the Southern Confederacy; it ends with the surrender of the Confederate army, led by General Robert E. Lee.

1861–65
Indiana fights for the Union in the Civil War.

1863
President Abraham Lincoln frees all slaves in the Southern Confederacy with the Emancipation Proclamation.

1889
Standard Oil decides to build a refinery in Whiting.

`1900`

1904
The Studebaker Manufacturing Company of South Bend produces its first gasoline-powered car.

1917–18
The United States engages in World War I.

U.S. Events

Indiana Events

1908
The U.S. Steel Corporation opens a mill in Gary.

1911
The first Indianapolis 500 race is held.

1929
The stock market crashes, plunging the United States more deeply into the Great Depression.

1933
About 25 percent of Hoosier workers are unemployed during the Great Depression.

1941–45
The United States engages in World War II.

1941–45
Indiana industries produce weapons and vehicles for use in World War II.

1951–53
The United States engages in the Korean War.

1959
Steel mills cut production by 90 percent following a strike.

1964–73
The United States engages in the Vietnam War.

1967
Richard G. Hatcher is elected the first black mayor of Gary.

1990s
Indiana's Hispanic population grows 117 percent.

1991
The United States and other nations engage in the brief Persian Gulf War against Iraq.

2000

2001
Terrorists hijack four U.S. aircraft and crash them into the World Trade Center in New York City, the Pentagon in Arlington, Virginia, and a Pennsylvania field, killing thousands.

Chief Justice John G. Roberts Jr.

2003
The United States and coalition forces invade Iraq.

2003
The Indiana Commission on Hispanic/Latino Affairs is created.

2005
Indiana native John G. Roberts Jr. becomes chief justice of the U.S. Supreme Court.

GLOSSARY

★ ★ ★

abolitionists people who work to end slavery

allies people who are on the same side in a conflict

appeal a legal proceeding in which a court is asked to change the decision of a lower court

archaeologists people who study the remains of past human societies

biodiesel fuel made from soybeans and diesel oil

biofuels energy sources made from plants or plant-derived materials

choreographers people who design the steps for a dance performance

civil involving a dispute between individuals

civil rights basic human rights that all citizens in a society are entitled to, such as the right to vote

confederation an association of groups that comes together with common goals

excavated removed soil and rock from an area to dig up buried items

frugal careful with money

interurbans small trains or trolley cars connecting two or more cities

petitions written calls for action, usually with signatures of people who support the action

probate court a court that deals with wills and the property of people who have died

Prohibition a legal ban on the making or sale of liquor

receded pulled or moved back over time

secede to withdraw from a group or an organization

sponsor act as a person who proposes or creates a bill

stalactites columns or pillars formed on the ceiling of a cave from dripping groundwater

stocks monetary investments in a company

strike an organized refusal to work, usually as a sign of protest about working conditions

toxicity the degree to which something is poisonous

tributary a smaller river that flows into a larger river

union an organization formed by workers to try to improve working conditions and wages

urban sprawl the spread of a city and its suburbs into rural areas

FAST FACTS

★ ★ ★

State Symbols

Statehood date	December 11, 1816, the 19th state
Origin of state name	Latin for "land of the Indians"
State capital	Indianapolis
State nickname	Hoosier State
State motto	"The Crossroads of America"
State bird	Cardinal
State flower	Peony
State tree	Tulip poplar (yellow poplar)
State stone	Limestone
State song	"On the Banks of the Wabash, Far Away"
State fair	Mid-August at Indianapolis

State seal

Geography

Total area; rank	36,418 square miles (94,322 sq km); 38th
Land; rank	35,867 square miles (92,895 sq km); 38th
Water; rank	551 square miles (1,427 sq km); 39th
Inland water; rank	316 square miles (818 sq km); 43rd
Great Lakes; rank	235 square miles (609 sq km); 8th
Geographic center	Boone County, 14 miles (23 km) north-northwest of Indianapolis
Latitude	37° 47' N to 41° 46' N
Longitude	84° 49' W to 88° 4' W
Highest point	Hoosier Hill, 1,257 feet (383 m), in Wayne County
Lowest point	Along the Ohio River, 320 feet (98 m)
Largest city	Indianapolis
Number of counties	92
Longest river	Wabash, 475 miles (764 km)

Population

Population; rank (2006 estimate)	6,313,520; 15th
Density (2006 estimate)	176 persons per square mile (68 per sq km)
Population distribution (2000 census)	71% urban, 29% rural
Ethnic distribution (2005 estimate)	White persons: 88.6%*
	Black persons: 8.8%*
	Asian persons: 1.2%*
	American Indian and Alaska Native persons: 0.3%*
	Native Hawaiian and Other Pacific Islanders: 0.0%*
	Persons reporting two or more races: 1.1%
	Persons of Hispanic or Latino origin: 4.5%†
	White persons not Hispanic: 84.3%

* Includes persons reporting only one race.
†Hispanics may be of any race, so they are also included in applicable race categories.

Weather

Record high temperature	116°F (47°C) at Collegeville on July 14, 1936
Record low temperature	−36°F (−38°C) at New Whiteland on January 19, 1994
Average July temperature	75°F (24°C)
Average January temperature	27°F (−3°C)
Average annual precipitation	40 inches (102 cm)

State flag

STATE SONG

★   ★   ★

"On the Banks of the Wabash, Far Away"

Words and music by Paul Dresser
The state legislature adopted this as the official song in 1913.

'Round my Indiana homestead wave the cornfields,
In the distance loom the woodlands clear and cool.
Oftentimes my thoughts revert to scenes of childhood,
Where I first received my lessons, nature's school.
But one thing there is missing in the picture,
Without her face it seems so incomplete,
I long to see my mother in the doorway,
As she stood there years ago, her boy to greet.

Chorus:
Oh, the moonlight's fair tonight along the Wabash,
From the fields there comes the breath of new-mown hay,
Through the sycamores the candle lights are gleaming,
On the banks of the Wabash, far away.

Many years have passed since I strolled by the river,
Arm in arm, with sweetheart Mary by my side,
It was there I tried to tell her that I loved her,
It was there I begged of her to be my bride.
Long years have passed since I strolled thro' the churchyard.
She's sleeping there, my angel, Mary dear,
I loved her, but she thought I didn't mean it,
Still I'd give my future were she only here.
(Chorus)

NATURAL AREAS AND HISTORIC SITES

National Memorial

Indiana's only national memorial is the *Lincoln Boyhood National Memorial*, which preserves the site where Abraham Lincoln lived between the ages of 7 and 21.

National Lakeshore

Indiana boasts a beautiful national lakeshore at the *Indiana Dunes National Lakeshore*. It is a great spot for hiking, swimming, biking, bird-watching, and wildlife viewing. Located on the southern shores of Lake Michigan, this lakeshore includes dunes, marshes, woodlands, a river, and a bog.

National Historical Park

The *George Rogers Clark National Historical Park* commemorates an event in 1779, in which frontiersmen led by Lieutenant Colonel George Rogers Clark captured the British fort formerly on this site, a charge that is still heralded as one of the great feats of the American Revolution.

National Forest

Hoosier National Forest in southern Indiana covers almost 200,000 acres (80,000 ha). It contains various smaller sites, including the Pioneer Mothers Memorial Forest, an old-growth forest; Hemlock Cliffs, which overlook a sandstone canyon; and Hickory Ridge Lookout Tower, which is listed on the National Historic Lookout Register.

State Parks and Forests

The Indiana State Park system maintains 24 state parks and recreation areas, including *Indiana Dunes State Park*, which features beautiful sand dune landscapes aside Lake Michigan; the *Falls of the Ohio State Park*, which features a fossil bedrock dating back millions of years; the *Spring Mill State Park*, which is home to a pioneer village with a historic gristmill; and *Whitewater Memorial State Park*, which was built as a World War II memorial.

SPORTS TEAMS

★ ★ ★

NCAA Teams (Division I)

Ball State University *Cardinals*
Butler University *Bulldogs*
Indiana State University *Sycamores*
Indiana University–Bloomington *Hoosiers*
Indiana University-Purdue University Fort Wayne *Mastodons*
Indiana University-Purdue University Indianapolis *Jaguars*
Purdue University *Boilermakers*
University of Evansville *Aces*
University of Notre Dame *Fighting Irish*
Valparaiso University *Crusaders*

PROFESSIONAL SPORTS TEAMS

★ ★ ★

National Basketball Association

Indiana *Pacers*

Women's National Basketball Association

Indiana *Fever*

National Football League

Indianapolis *Colts*

CULTURAL INSTITUTIONS

★ ★ ★

Libraries

The *Indiana State Library* has information on the history of the state and its citizens, along with genealogical records for family history research.

The *Indiana University-Purdue University Indianapolis Library* includes a special philanthropic library, as well as government statistics, information on the state, and general collections.

Opened in the late 19th century, the *Willard Library* in Evansville is Indiana's oldest public library building. It includes the Thrall Art Book Collection and a rich supply of genealogical resources.

Museums

The *General Lew Wallace Study & Museum* (Crawfordsville) contains items collected by Wallace during his life as an author, soldier, statesman, artist, violinist, and inventor.

The *Great Lakes Museum of Military History* (Michigan City) contains rare documents, old military uniforms, medals, and weapons used in combat.

The *Indiana Railway Museum* (French Lick) gives train rides through parts of Hoosier National Forest, including one of the longest railroad tunnels in Indiana.

The *Indiana State Museum* (Indianapolis) contains a wealth of information on the state, such as radio and television broadcast history, sports history, and prehistoric exhibits.

The *Indianapolis Museum of Art* is the seventh-largest art museum in the country. Lush gardens surround the building.

The Lincoln Museum (Fort Wayne) is dedicated to a collection of Abraham Lincoln artifacts and art.

Performing Arts

Indiana has one major opera company, two major symphony orchestras, and one major dance company.

Universities and Colleges

In 2006, Indiana had 30 public and 69 private institutions of higher learning.

ANNUAL EVENTS

January–March

Winter sports in LaPorte and New Carlisle (January and February)

Parke County Maple Syrup Fair in Rockville (February–March)

Indiana High School Athletic Association State Basketball Tournament in Indianapolis (March)

April–June

Mushroom Festival in Mansfield (April)

Sugar Creek Canoe Race in Crawfordsville (April)

Tulipfest in Bloomington (April)

Marion Easter Pageant (April or May)

Indianapolis 500 Race and Festival (Memorial Day weekend)

Bluegrass Music Festival in Beanblossom (June)

Festival of the Arts and Crafts in Lowell (June)

Glass Festival in Greentown (June)

Miss Indiana Pageant in Michigan City (June)

July–September

Freedom Festival in Evansville (June and July)

Circus City Festival in Peru (July)

Hydroplane Regatta in Madison (July)

Indiana State Fair in Indianapolis (August)

National Muzzle Loading Rifle Association Championship Shoot in Friendship (August)

Daviess County Turkey Trot Festival (September)

October–December

Harvest Homecoming in New Albany (October)

Parke County Covered Bridge Festival in Rockville (October)

Indianapolis Christmas Lighting Ceremony (November and December)

Traditional Christmas at the Conner Prairie Pioneer Settlement (November and December)

Indiana Day across the state (December 11)

BIOGRAPHICAL DICTIONARY

Albion Fellows Bacon (1865–1933) of Evansville was a writer and social reformer. The Albion Fellows Bacon Center to prevent domestic abuse was named in her honor.

David Nathaniel Baker (1931–) is an award-winning jazz musician, professor, and chair of the Jazz Department at Indiana University School of Music in Bloomington.

Anne Baxter (1923–1985) starred in films such as *All About Eve* and *The Ten Commandments*. She was born in Michigan City.

Evan Bayh (1955–) served as Indiana's governor from 1988 to 1997 and was elected to the U.S. Senate in 1999.

Joshua Bell (1967–) is an award-winning violinist. He was born in Bloomington.

Larry Bird See page 77.

Frank Borman (1928–), a native of Gary, served as an astronaut in the Apollo space program. With two other astronauts, he made the first flight around the moon.

Norman Bridwell (1928–) is a children's book author and illustrator who developed Clifford the Big Red Dog. He was born in Kokomo.

Robert Lee Brokenburr (1886–1974), a lawyer, was the first African American elected to the Indiana state senate (served 1941–1944).

Dorothy Richard Buell See page 21.

Norman Bridwell

Hoagland "Hoagy" Carmichael (1899–1981) composed popular songs from the 1920s through the 1950s, including hits such as "Stardust" and "In the Cool, Cool, Cool of the Evening." He was born in Bloomington.

Julia M. Carson See page 86.

Oscar Charleston (1896–1954) was a baseball player in the Negro Leagues. He was inducted into the Baseball Hall of Fame in 1976. Indianapolis was his hometown.

George Rogers Clark (1752–1818) was a lieutenant colonel in the Virginia militia during the American Revolution. He played a big part in winning the Northwest Territory for the United States.

Oscar Charleston

Levi Coffin See page 50.

Jim Davis (1945–), a native of Marion, draws the cartoon cat Garfield. He based his cartoon character on a grouchy cat that lived on his family farm.

James Dean (1931–1955), an actor, starred in the films *East of Eden* and *Rebel Without a Cause*. He was born in Marion.

Eugene V. Debs See page 52.

Theodore Dreiser (1871–1945), who was born in Terre Haute, was a writer. His first great novel was *Sister Carrie*.

Shirley Graham Du Bois (1896–1977) was an African American playwright and biographer of great African Americans such as Phillis Wheatley and Frederick Douglass. She was born in Evansville.

William Forsyth (1854–1935) was a painter in a movement called the Hoosier School. He founded an art school in Muncie and taught at the John Herron Art Institute in Indianapolis.

Vivica A. Fox (1964–) of South Bend is a popular motion picture and television actress.

Crystal Gayle (1951–), born in Kentucky but raised in Indiana, is a country music star famous for the hit song "Don't It Make My Brown Eyes Blue."

William Auge "Will" Geer (1902–1978) was an actor who is best remembered for his role as the grandpa in the 1970s TV series *The Waltons*. He was born in Frankfort.

Ron Glass (1945–), who was born in Evansville, played roles in a number of television sitcoms. His most famous role was as Detective Ron Harris on *Barney Miller*, which aired in the 1970s and 1980s.

Virgil "Gus" Grissom

Virgil "Gus" Grissom (1926–1967), a native of Mitchell, was one of the original astronauts selected in 1959 for the U.S. space program and the second U.S. astronaut to fly in space.

Johnny Gruelle (1880–1938) was a cartoonist who designed the Raggedy Ann doll. He went on to create the Raggedy Ann and Andy series of children's books. He grew up in Indianapolis.

Charles "Buster" Hall (1920–1971) was the first African American aviator to shoot down a German warplane during World War II. He was from Brazil, Indiana.

Katie B. Hall (1938–) was the first African American woman from Indiana elected to the U.S. House of Representatives (1982–1985).

Benjamin Harrison See page 88.

William Henry Harrison See page 88.

Richard G. Hatcher See page 63.

Florence Henderson (1934–), who was born in Dale, is an actress and singer. She played Carol Brady in TV's *The Brady Bunch*, a successful sitcom that ran from 1969 to 1974.

Theodore M. Hesburgh (1917–) is a Roman Catholic priest, educator, and writer who was president of the University of Notre Dame from 1952 to 1987.

Felrath Hines (1913–1933) was an African American civil rights activist and artist.

James Hoffa (1913–?), a native of Brazil, Indiana, was a controversial labor leader. He disappeared in 1975 and was never seen again. He was declared dead in 1982.

Robert Indiana (1928–), who was born Robert Clark in New Castle, is a sculptor who makes pop artwork out of letters and numbers.

Janet Jackson (1966–) is a pop music star and member of the Jackson family of musicians that includes brother Michael and sister La Toya. She is from Gary.

Janet Jackson

Michael Jackson (1958–), who is from Gary, first sang with his four older brothers in a group called the Jackson 5. In 1979, his first solo album, *Off the Wall*, became the first record to chart four top-10 hits.

Annie Fellows Johnston (1863–1931) was a children's book author who invented a young girl nicknamed the Little Colonel. Johnston grew up in McCutchanville.

Percy Julian See page 73.

Greg Kinnear (1963–) is a television talk show host and actor who has appeared in many films, including *As Good As It Gets* and *Little Miss Sunshine*. He was born in Logansport.

René-Robert Cavelier, Sieur de La Salle See page 35.

David Letterman (1947–), a native of Indianapolis, is a comedian and television talk show host. Since 1993, he has hosted the *Late Show with David Letterman*.

Eli Lilly See page 99.

Abraham Lincoln See page 88.

Carole Lombard (1908–1942), born Jane Alice Peters in Fort Wayne, was an actor in such films as *Mr. & Mrs. Smith* and *To Be or Not to Be*.

Shelley Long (1949–) is an actor and screenwriter best known for her role in the TV comedy *Cheers* during the 1980s. She is from Fort Wayne.

Richard Green Lugar (1932–) has been a U.S. senator from Indiana since 1977. Before being elected to the Senate, he was mayor of Indianapolis from 1968 to 1975.

Karl Malden (1912–) is a stage and screen actor whose movies include *On the Waterfront* and *A Streetcar Named Desire* for which he won an Oscar. He grew up in Gary.

Steve McQueen (1930–1980), born in Beech Grove, was an actor of the 1960s and 1970s. One of his biggest hits was the film *Bullitt*.

John Mellencamp (1951–) is a rock singer and songwriter. Early in his career, he performed as John Cougar. He was born in Seymour.

John Mellencamp

Dale Messick (1906–2005), from South Bend, created a comic strip about a newspaper reporter named Brenda Starr.

Jane Pauley (1950–), a native of Indianapolis, cohosted NBC's *Today* show in the 1970s and 1980s. She then created the feature news program that became *Dateline*.

Bill Peet (1915–2002), born William Bartlett Peet in Grandview, was a screenwriter, cartoonist, and the author and illustrator of 35 children's books. He wrote the screenplay for *101 Dalmatians*.

Sydney Pollack (1934–), born in Lafayette, is a film director and producer. In 1986, he won Oscars for Best Picture and Best Director for *Out of Africa*.

Jane Pauley

Pontiac See page 38.

Cole Porter See page 74.

Ernie Pyle See page 109.

James Whitcomb Riley See page 70.

John G. Roberts Jr. See page 87.

Oscar Robertson See page 79.

Knute Rockne See page 59.

William M. Scholl (1882–1968), better known as "Dr. Scholl," developed foot-care products.

May Wright Sewall (1844–1920) worked to help women gain the right to vote. She also founded a school for girls in Indianapolis.

Jean Shepherd (1921–1999) was a radio personality, short-story writer, and screenwriter who wrote the movie *A Christmas Story* based on his childhood in Hammond.

Red Skelton (1913–1997) was a popular radio and television comedian from Vincennes. From 1951 to 1971, he had his own TV show.

Theodore Clement Steele (1847–1926) was a painter who belonged to the Hoosier School. Admirers especially treasure his depiction of natural light in landscape paintings.

George P. Stewart (1874–1924) helped found the *Indianapolis Recorder* in the 1890s. This newspaper for African Americans is still published today.

Twyla Tharp

Gene Stratton-Porter (1863–1924) was an author and photographer. Her novel *Freckles* is set in central Indiana. She was born in Wabash County.

Twyla Tharp (1941–) is a dancer, director, and choreographer who has won Tony and Emmy awards. She was born in Portland.

Tara VanDerveer See page 78.

Kurt Vonnegut Jr. (1922–2007) wrote satirical novels, often with a science-fiction twist, including *Slaughterhouse Five*. He was from Indianapolis.

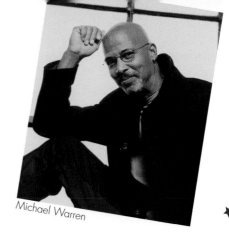
Michael Warren

Madam C. J. Walker See page 55.

Lew Wallace (1827–1905) was a Union army colonel and lawyer who wrote *Ben-Hur*, a historical novel set in the time of the ancient Roman empire. He was born in Brookville.

Michael Warren (1946–) is an actor best known for his role as officer Bobby Hill in the 1980s TV crime series *Hill Street Blues*. He was born in South Bend.

Marie D. Webster (1859–1956) wrote *Quilts: Their Story and How to Make Them* (1915). She is a member of the Quilters Hall of Fame, and her home in Marion is its headquarters.

Jessamyn West (1902–1984) wrote stories about the Quakers in Indiana. Her best-known stories are *The Friendly Persuasion* and *Except for Me and Thee*.

Ryan White (1971–1990) was a Kokomo teenager and activist who worked to end discrimination against people with AIDS.

Robert Wise (1914–2005) was an Academy Award–winning producer and director of such films as *The Sound of Music* and *West Side Story*. He was born in Winchester.

Wilbur Wright (1867–1912), with his brother Orville, invented and flew the first airplane. Wilbur was born in Millville.

RESOURCES

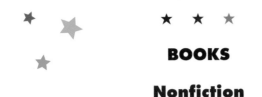

BOOKS

Nonfiction

Aller, Susan Bivin. *Tecumseh*. Minneapolis: Lerner Publishing Group, 2004.

Boomhower, Ray E. *The Sword and Pen: A Life of Lew Wallace*. Indianapolis: Indiana Historical Society, 2005.

Gallant, Roy A. *Sand on the Move: The Story of Dunes*. Danbury, Conn.: Franklin Watts, 1998.

Pimm, Nancy Roe. *Indy 500: The Inside Track*. Plain City, Ohio: Darby Creek Publishing, 2004.

Stewart, Mark, and Matt Zyesing. *The Indiana Pacers*. Chicago: Norwood House Press, 2007.

Wilkie, Katharine E., and Cathy Morrison (illustrator). *George Rogers Clark: Boy of the Northwest Frontier*. Indianapolis: Patria Press, 2004.

Williams, Jean Kinney. *Benjamin Harrison*. Danbury, Conn.: Scholastic Library Publishing, 2004.

Fiction

Homan, Lynn M., Thomas Reilly, and Rosalie Shepherd (illustrator). *The Tuskegee Airmen Story*. Gretna, La.: Pelican Publishing Company, 2002.

Johnston, Annie Fellows. *The Little Colonel*. Illustrated Edition. Bel Air, Calif.: Dodo Press, 2006.

Peet, Bill. *The Whingdingdilly*. Boston: Houghton Mifflin, 1982.

Riley, James Whitcomb. *Little Orphant Annie and Other Poems*. Mineola, N.Y.: Dover Publications, 1994.

Stratton-Porter, Gene. *Freckles*. Winnetka, Calif.: Norilana Books, 2006.

Thrasher, Crystal. *The Dark Didn't Catch Me*. Bloomington: Indiana University Press, 2004.

DVDs

The Artists of Brown County. Quarry Books, 1994.
A Christmas Story. Warner Home Video, 2006.
The History of Indiana Basketball. Warner Home Video, 2007.
Indianapolis 500: The Legacy Series. Studio Works, 2005.
NFL Films: Colts: The Complete History. Warner Home Video, 2006.
The Tuskegee Airmen. HBO Home Video, 2001.
Young Lincoln: The Early Life of Abraham Lincoln, 1816–1830. FYI Productions, 2005.

WEB SITES AND ORGANIZATIONS

Conner Prairie History Online

www.connerprairie.org/discover_learn/ historyonline
For articles, primary sources, and bibliographies on a wide range of topics in 19th-century Indiana history.

Indiana County History Preservation Society

www.countyhistory.com
A county-by-county collection of articles, images, maps, and biographies concerning Indiana pioneers and early settlers.

Indiana Geological Survey

http://igs.indiana.edu/geology/topo/ landscapes/index.cfm
Interactive maps, diagrams, articles, FAQs, a glossary, and a visual dictionary presented by Indiana University.

Indiana Historical Bureau

www.in.gov/history
To find articles, primary source documents and artifacts, FAQs, state symbols, and more relating to Indiana history.

Indiana Magazine of History

www.indiana.edu/~imaghist/index.html
To find articles, primary source documents, and links to related Web sites, published by the Indiana University Department of History in cooperation with the Indiana Historical Society.

Indianapolis 500

www.indy500.com
To find out the history, traditions, facts, and statistics related to the Indy 500.

Northern Indiana Center for History

www.centerforhistory.org/indiana_history_ maincontents.html
Statewide facts, statistics, symbols, and chronological history articles, as well as information on African American and Polish American experiences in St. Joseph.

INDEX

★ ★ ★

AUTHOR'S TIPS AND SOURCE NOTES

★ ★ ★

A lot of credit for preserving the Hoosier heritage goes to the Indiana Historical Society in Indianapolis. Its online materials, reading recommendations, and publications, such as *Indiana: A New Historical Guide* by Robert M. Taylor Jr., have been very valuable in researching this book. Other books, such as *Indiana Trivia* by Ernie and Jill Couch and *Oddball Indiana* by Jerome Pohlen, have provided facts on the lighter side. The Michigan City Public Library has a wealth of information about the German immigrants who came to the area in the 1800s. Finally, much thanks goes to helpful Hoosiers, such as the folks at the statehouse and in the office of the Indianapolis mayor, who took the time to answer my questions and help me fill in the blanks.